Communicating Successfully in Groups

Communicating Successfully in Groups is a practical guide to effective communication, suitable for anyone for whom communication in groups is a key part of their job. *Marie Reid* and *Richard Hammersley* uniquely draw together both theory and practice from psychology, sociology and business studies in an accessible and straightforward manner. They give practical advice and exercises useful for both personal development and for improving professional skills.

Suitable as an introduction for psychology students, *Communicating Successfully in Groups* will be invaluable for students of business, medicine, allied health professions, social work and social policy, whether studying on a short course or attending an intensive training session as part of their continuing professional development.

Marie Reid is Senior Lecturer in Social Psychology at the University of Wales, Swansea. **Richard Hammersley** is Professor of Social Psychology also at the University of Wales, Swansea. They have both taught communication skills to a wide variety of students and health professionals over many years.

Communicating Successfully in Groups

A practical guide for the workplace

**Marie Reid and
Richard Hammersley**

London and Philadelphia

First published 2000
by Routledge
11 New Fetter Lane, London EC4P 4EE

Simultaneously published in the USA and Canada
by Taylor and Francis Inc
325 Chestnut Street, Philadelphia, PA 19106

Routledge is an imprint of the Taylor & Francis Group

© 2000 Marie Reid and Richard Hammersley

Typeset in Goudy by
Florence Production Ltd, Stoodleigh, Devon
Printed and bound in Great Britain by
TJ International Ltd, Padstow, Cornwall

British Library Cataloguing in Publication Data
A catalogue record for this book is available
from the British Library

Library of Congress Cataloguing in Publication Data
Reid, Marie, 1967–
     Communicating successfully in groups: a practical guide for the workplace/
Marie Reid and Richard Hammersley.
          p. cm.
     Includes bibliographical references and index.
     1. Interpersonal communication. I. Hammersley, Richard. II. Title.
HM1166.R45 2000
302.3'5--dc21   99–057361

ISBN 0–415–20102–0 (hbk)
ISBN 0–415–20103–9 (pbk)

For Suzanna Hammersley without whom this book would have been written more quickly but with less love and happiness.

Contents

Tables

Acknowledgements

This book is based on our teaching practice and we would like to thank the many students we have taught communication to over the years for their enthusiasm and feedback. We also owe a great debt to the many authors whose ideas we have paraphrased, we hope without ruining them in the process.

1 Welcome to group communication in the workplace

What is this book for?

If you are looking at this book then we assume that you are interested in how groups function at work and in learning *how* to communicate more effectively in them. As we will see, group communication is central to and essential for most modern work. Good group communication is not easy to achieve, requires skill and attention, often goes wrong and is fundamentally *intersubjective*, which we will explain shortly. The two main aims of this book are:

1 To provide an understanding of the nature and functioning of groups at work.
2 To provide suggestions that will help you to improve your group communication skills at work and deal more effectively with problems.

We hope that the book provides an accessible introduction to group communication in the workplace, which is readable without being simplistic.

Who is this book for?

Anybody who is involved in groups in their workplace, which means almost anyone who works. This includes people who work in business, health care, education, social services and criminal justice. We believe that there are general principles and skills for group communication that apply to all workplaces and will date quite slowly. In contrast, specific advice about, say, building a health care team, or a tele-sales operation, will tend to date quite quickly as technology and current practices change.

Intersubjectivity

All communication is intersubjective – involving exchange between two or more people – but the difficulties of intersubjectivity are particularly serious for group communication. Many books on communication list simple techniques that are likely – but not guaranteed – to have specific effects on another person. Effects on group communication are less predictable for two reasons. First, because everybody involved in a group has an effect on the group dynamics, which in turn affects how the group members behave. The more people are involved, the more difficult it will be to understand the group, control it, or predict how it will turn out.

Second, because the nature of social interactions is fundamentally open, rather than being fixed by unchanging laws of psychology or biology. For a start, people can and do read books like this one, then modify their behaviour in groups, changing how the groups function. The current popularity of management teams has altered how many workplaces are organised and how groups are likely to interact. By comparison, the basics of how two people talk to each other remain fairly constant whatever their knowledge, social setting and culture.

A third aspect of intersubjectivity is that all the people involved in a group communication come to it with equal rights and responsibilities as people. In consequence, effective group communication requires flexibility, the ability to adapt to changing circumstances and the ability to communicate openly with other people. It is not possible to write out a simple list of effective group communication techniques, to be applied to all situations.

Objectives of this book

The book can be divided into three parts. The first part (Chapters 2–4) covers basic communication skills. Chapter 2 looks at the basic nature of interpersonal communication. It covers the difficulties of defining 'excellent interpersonal skills', the different channels of communication that are used, the differences between literal or denotative, connotative, action and social meaning, and how the formality of a social setting is indicated. Chapter 3 looks at non-verbal channels of communication and covers the different channels, the idea of leakage in communication, the presentation of self in the workplace and suggests methods for improving non-verbal communication. Chapter 4 goes on to look at verbal communication, covering questioning, listening and acknowledging emotions and feelings, self-disclosure and assertiveness.

The second part (Chapters 5–8) looks at the nature of social inter-action and how and why groups come together and function. Chapter 5 discusses the myths of personal identity, suggesting that personal identity is socially-constructed and that people are different in different social situations. It covers five-factor personality theory, problems with the dualist view of there being a stable 'self' independent of actual social behaviour, and looks at the communication difficulties that can arise by assuming a stable self. Chapter 6 goes on to look at the social construction of identity. It proposes that: identity is fluid, dynamic and negotiable; identity is communicative; we signify our social iden-tities to other people, interpret feedback from them about what we are like and may modify our identities on the basis of that feedback; our stable personal identities are constructed to make sense of what has happened to us and how we have related to other people; people's identity constructs are usually socially functional for them, and this can apply even to deviant, damaged or spoiled identities; identity involves identification with specific groups of people, but also contri-bution to the nature of those groups – this is a fundamental aspect of social activity; people routinely adopt different identities in different social groups – hence the idea of a social role. Chapter 7 looks at how groups form. It emphasises the importance of groups at work, covers different stage models of group formation, as well as the main psychodynamic theories of groups. It looks at group cohesion, formal and informal norms and at the importance of open communication in groups. Chapter 8 looks at social influence in groups, covering the main forms of social power, the nature of authority and leadership and the main mechanisms of social influence, which include normal-isation, conformity, obedience and de-individuation.

The third part (Chapters 9–12) looks at the functioning of groups in the workplace. Chapter 9 looks at decision-making in groups. It first examines the advantages of group decision-making then looks at the main problems that can occur, including risky shift, polarisation and groupthink. It looks at the group processes that underlie decision-making, some common traps and how to avoid them, it also suggests some techniques for making better decisions in groups. Chapter 10 looks at working beyond the group, covering negotiation and conflict resolution, as well as some of the problems and difficulties that can arise in inter-group and inter-agency working. Chapter 11 looks in detail at the workplace team, examining the importance of teams, different roles within a team, how to build a team and get it to work effectively, why teams can be dysfunctional and some of the disad-vantages of team work. Chapter 12 looks forward into the twenty-first century and the nature of group communication in a network society. It sketches how work has changed in network society, relying more upon electronic communications, looks at how communication works in cyberspace, provides some advice for communicating effectively there and suggests a continued need for face-to-face groups at work.

Finally, Chapter 13 provides a brief summing up.

How we wrote this book

The book is based on our teaching of communication to a variety of student and professional groups. We have drawn upon three types of information. First, there is a research literature in social psychology that looks at how groups work, often by conducting experiments that manipulate group behaviour to see what happens. While this research has been criticised as being artificial, some of the main phenomena discovered appear to apply also to real workplaces. However, we feel that previous books on group communication have tended to rely too much on this literature and over-emphasise theoretical details at the expense of practical advice. Second, there is a large literature in management and organisational psychology, as well as psychotherapy, describing how groups and teams function, as well as prescribing how they should function. This literature can be criticised for having a weak evidence base. Some ideas are well-researched, some are based on extensive work and observation in real organisations and groups, but many ideas seem to have been invented by the authors. Third, we draw also upon our own experiences working and teaching in large organisations – universities in our case. While we also may be criticised for invention, we hope that drawing upon our own experiences brings the more academic material to life.

What is good group communication?

We shall deal with this in more detail throughout the book, but it is worthwhile to take a minute or two to reflect on what *good group communication* means to you. Write down some phrases or words that spring to mind. Compare your list with ours:

- Speaking well in groups, and listening to others effectively.
- Observing communication between others in the group.
- Understanding ourselves and our relationships with others in the groups that we belong to.
- Getting on well as a group.

- Making sound decisions quickly as a group.
- Providing emotional support for each other.
- Acquiring key communication skills to make the group function more effectively; offering praise, helping the group to relax, sharing ideas and information, inviting opinions, summarising ideas and information, suggesting action.

Can group communication skills be learned?

You may think that you already have good communication skills based on how you communicate with friends and family and that you should therefore have no problems in dealing with colleagues in a group setting. However, an individual's communicative style may differ depending on the situation and set of expectations that he/she takes along to the situation. For example, meeting as part of a group in the pub with close friends is completely different from a business meeting with colleagues, which means your behaviour and communicative style will also be different. A word of caution: it is often those who are overly confident who tend to be the least competent at communicating in groups.

There is clear evidence that communication skills can and should be learned. The need to acquire these skills is becoming more and more a priority in undergraduate courses ranging from degrees in business to degrees in medicine. We hope this book will help you develop such skills or improve on existing skills. There is evidence that students learn communication skills most effectively if the following conditions are met:

- Specific tasks are set and instructions are provided on how to practice skills.
- Students are given the opportunities to practise these skills in real life settings or in role play scenarios.
- Feedback is provided on performance (it is helpful if positive feedback is provided before negative).
- Self-monitoring is used (e.g., use of audio or video tape, self assessment exercises, constant self reflection).

It is obvious, then, that a book alone cannot improve communication skills. The ideal use of this book is as background reading for a specific training on group communication at work. It is also possible for the reader to use the book to design their own self-instruction programme. To do this you would have to work with others so that practice and feedback can be obtained. The exercises at the end of each chapter are designed with this in mind.

What is a group?

Finally, it is appropriate to introduce groups. What does the word 'group' mean to you? It might be worthwhile jotting down a definition of a group and the purpose of a group before you read on.

You may have discovered that defining the word 'group' is not so simple. Group behaviour is often different from the sum of individual behaviours. A collection of people is not necessarily a group. A group presumes communication within the group. The word 'group' can carry many different meanings and associations. Different types of group have different functions and qualities. Some groups are formal (a class, a committee meeting, an annual general meeting, a conference presentation), some are informal (friends in the pub, the family holidays). Some groups are reasonably stable and long lasting (family, school), others are more short-lived (party gathering, conference). Some groups are highly organised (Scouts or Guides), others are barely organised at all (skate boarders on their favourite steps). Some groups are small in size (4–5 people), others are large (several hundred). Some are local, others are international. It would seem that the key component is that there is some common interest or purpose that brings them together. Sherif and Sherif (1969) believed that the key component to groups was the *presence of a social structure*, generally in the form of *status* and *role relationships*. The family is a good example of a group with implicit social structure, as each member has very well defined relationships with each other and with these relationships normally come clear roles and status differences.

Harré and Lamb (1986) provide a dictionary definition of a group as:

> Two or more persons who are interacting with one another, who share a set of common goals and norms which direct their activities, and who develop a set of roles and a network of affective relations.

This definition refers more to small groups or 'face-to face' groups of about three to eight people such as family, social and working-group relationships rather than larger groups such as the members of the Labour Party. Smaller groups are the specific focus of this book.

Recommended general textbooks

Adler, R.B and Towne, N. (1993) *Looking Out / Looking In*, seventh edition, Fort Worth: Harcourt Brace Jovanovich.

Dimbleby, R. and Burton, G. (1992) *More Than Words. An Introduction to Communication*, second edition, London: Routledge.

Forgas, J. P. (1986) *Interpersonal Behaviour; The Psychology of Social Interaction*, Sydney: Pergamon Press.

Hargie, O.D.W. (1997) *The Handbook of Communication skills*, second edition, Routledge, London.

Harré, R. and Lamb, R. (eds) (1986) *The Dictionary of Personality and Social Psychology*, Oxford: Blackwell.

Hartley, P. (1997) *Group Communication*, London: Routledge.

2 The nature of interpersonal communication

Thinking about communication

In almost any job it will help to have 'excellent interpersonal skills' as they say in the job adverts. This chapter will look at the nature of interpersonal communication and at what makes for excellent communication in groups. Being able to communicate well with people is important for communicating with colleagues, for dealing with clients or customers, for managing people and for training or teaching people. The chapter will then move on to look at the social meanings of communication.

Objectives

By the end of the chapter you should:

- Appreciate the difficulties of defining 'excellent interpersonal skills'.
- Know the different channels of communication that are used.
- Understand the differences between literal or denotative, connotative, action and social meaning.
- Know how the formality of a social setting is indicated.

What are 'excellent interpersonal skills'?

Reading job specifications, such skills in the workplace are often reduced to a series of platitudes and clichés. Here are some common ones:

- Able to work in a team.
- Able to communicate at the highest level (or all levels).

- Pleasant manner.
- Lively and outgoing personality.
- Able to manage a large and diverse team.
- Able to sell.

What do these phrases actually mean? Take a moment to think over what kinds of job you would associate with these different phrases.

Is it feasible that the same core skills will enable people to do all these things?

The answer is yes, for skilled communicators will generally be able to adapt their interpersonal skills as appropriate for the particular situation.

To illustrate this point, let us divide people into three levels of communication skill:

1   The 'natural' who simply use whatever methods come naturally to them, for good or bad. They will tend to have relatively little insight into how their communication skills affect other people and may be resistant to improving. They may be inclined to blame other people for communication failures, or to dismiss themselves as hopeless and unchangeable. Alternatively, if they have succeeded with their natural skills, then they may believe that they communicate in the only proper way. In the workplace, naturals will do all right in some jobs, but fail in others where different skills are required. For example, rude bullies often get their own way with gentler people. This teaches them that rudeness and bullying are successful and they may believe that people who do not behave like that are wimps. However, unbeknown to the rude bully, such unpleasant behaviour makes other people avoid them as much as possible. The rude bully may end up socially isolated, with the actual workings of the social or workplace group largely concealed from him or her. This applies even to the boss. Berate your staff too much and they will learn to conceal their work from you, bringing you only rosy and unrealistic reports. Think of the Soviet dictator Stalin, perhaps the ultimate rude bully, and the fact that nobody dared report failure to him, for fear of severe punishment.
2   The 'tricky', who have learned certain useful communication skills, but who have difficulty applying them in all social situations. They tend to have a limited range of communication skills tricks, that work in some situations but fail in others. For example, some

unassertive people will not openly tell other people what they want to happen, because they fear conflict. Instead, they drop broad hints, such as sighing when you pass by their desk in the hope that you will offer to help them. This technique will work in interactions with socially skilled, sensitive people, but will fail with people who do not notice the person's hints, or who are willing to ignore them. Sometimes a more direct approach is necessary, even at the risk of conflict.

Even communication techniques that are good generally can be tiresome if applied in all situations. We have all met 'good listeners' from the caring professions who will display appropriate signs of interest in what someone else is saying, even when their minds are a thousand miles away. Tactfully admitting lack of interest can be an appropriate communication skill!

3   The 'skilful', who have a wide range of communication skills that they can use appropriately whatever the social situation. For example, a truly skilful communicator will be able to judge when it is appropriate to behave like a rude bully, perhaps to nip another person's bad behaviour in the bud, when it is appropriate to drop hints, perhaps when the other person is overly-sensitive, and when some other strategy is appropriate. Nobody lives up to this high standard all the time, whatever is on their mind, particularly if they feel anxious, ill, depressed or worried at the time.

'Excellent interpersonal skills' involve:

Learning; the ability to observe, evaluate and change how you communicate with other people. This requires self-awareness, as well as a willingness to respond to feedback from others and to recognise shortcomings.

Techniques; knowing and being able to use appropriate communication skills techniques. Many short courses perhaps over-emphasise these techniques, as if they were tricks that could be applied without further thought. Nonetheless, basic techniques can be of great help.

Flexibility; being able to judge and learn when which skills are appropriate. Listening skills are of no use when you have to do a presentation, while being highly articulate is of little use when someone wants you to recognise their feelings.

Knowledge is a further dimension. Knowing how people communicate with each other allows you to become more aware of communicative processes as they occur and hence learn more quickly.

Common objections to learning communication skills

That 'touchy-feely' stuff wastes time that I could spend more profitably

Poor communication is indeed a big waste of time, but effective communication saves time. A boss who barks orders that underlings are afraid to question is wasting time because the orders may be unclear, or impossible to carry out. The boss may save time talking, but the employees will waste much more time trying to carry out (or pretending to carry out) unclear or impossible orders. Other time wasters are people who talk too long or repeat themselves. This is usually because they are not being listened to effectively. For example, someone may make a point because they want to have their feelings recognised and accepted by the group. If their feelings are ignored, then they will tend to bring up the same sort of point repeatedly, or go on at length. This sort of activity is common in committees! Time can be saved with effective listening. Customers who complain are often satisfied if their feelings are recognised and acknowledged, but may take the matter further if they are not. For example, patients who sue doctors have usually not had their feelings about their maltreatment acknowledged by medical staff, who have instead tried to minimise the problems, or deny responsibility.

Communication should be natural and unforced

Even if this were true in one's social life (and it is not – just think of the lengths people will go to in order to present themselves in a good light to a new love), there is nothing 'natural' or 'unforced' about modern work. For most of the length of human history, most people lived in small communities where everyone knew each other. In contrast, the modern workplace involves interacting with dozens, hundreds, even thousands of people, most of whom you will barely get to know. Once you have worked for years with someone, you may naturally come to understand each other's 'little ways' and get along very well. These days there is rarely the time for this. For example, in most jobs involving sales you may deal with hundreds of people a day; sometimes several at once.

I communicate perfectly well already

Most people indeed have some good communication skills. Unfortunately, most people tend to over-rate their own skill and to ignore areas of weakness. Someone who is an articulate and forceful speaker may fail to recognise that she is a poor listener and bad at attending to non-verbal cues from her colleagues that she has gone on for too long. On the other hand, someone who listens well may find it difficult to speak up and may fail to realise the messages conveyed by their body language. We remember Professor Shanks, who spent an entire hour's meeting speaking, while everyone else tried to look interested because he was head of department. He posed a number of questions about what should be done, paused for a few seconds then answered himself. At the end he said, 'Well, that was a good discussion', and seemed rather satisfied. Needless to say none of the ideas he mentioned were ever put into practice.

It is also worth saying that few of us have the skill (and nerve) to communicate well in all social situations. For example, most of us have had male colleagues who communicate well with other men, but are less comfortable communicating with women. Even unusually skilled communicators can make surprising fools of themselves when put on the spot by someone of high social status, or by someone they find attractive.

In communication, it is tempting to blame others for the problems that occur. For example, when an employee and their line manager are having problems, each often blames the other. One common miscommunication can occur when the manager has expected the employee to raise problems, while the employee has expected the manager to actively ask about problems.

The appropriate starting place is to learn to communicate effectively oneself. This and the next chapter simply provide an overview. There are many excellent books on general communication skills, some of which are listed at the end of the chapter.

The nature of communication

The rest of this chapter describes the nature of communication. If you have read or been trained on communication skills then this will be familiar to you. The chapter will use examples, but we must emphasise that communication is an open, creative activity and, despite what you read in magazines, it is not possible to give simple checklists such as 'How to recognise aggression at work' or 'Ten ways to flirt with your colleagues'.

Communication between people involves the exchange of information

Different kinds of communication can be used to inform:

- language, including speech (not forgetting sign language), writing, other codes – such as semaphore or pictograms;
- paralanguage, including intonation, accent and tone of voice;
- facial expressions;
- gestures;
- body movement and posture;
- non-linguistic styles, including the choice of medium: face-to-face, telephone, e-mail, fax, letter, memo, etc.;
- personal appearance and clothing;
- scent;
- the decoration and design of the environment; and
- the style and nature of any audio-visual aids, including things like handwriting.

Communication between people can involve a lot of information, through some or all these different channels. Most people use all these channels to some extent, but few people do so skilfully and it is probably impossible to be aware of all the information being conveyed all of the time. For simplicity, this section will focus on face-to-face verbal communications, but many of the points apply to written communication and to other media.

Key communication skills that can be learned

- Listening
- Observing paralanguage and non-linguistic information
- Interpreting meanings on the basis of all information
- Speaking
- Monitoring and controlling the non-verbal information that you present
- Impression management

Some of these skills will be dealt with in Chapters 3 and 4. First, we will look at the meanings and functions of language and how these relate to the social situation where communication is occurring.

Language

The meanings of language

Most of the time we understand what people say without much effort, but this does not mean that understanding language is straightforward. It is useful to consider four different types of meaning, which together communicate our understanding of spoken or written (or indeed signed) language.

Literal meanings

The literal meaning of an utterance is what it would mean if you looked it up word-for-word in a dictionary then applied the rules of grammar to it. According to literal meaning the correct answer to 'Can you pass the salt?' is 'Yes, I am able to', but this is not what it is meant to mean. The utterance is intended to mean 'Would you pass me the salt, please', and most of the time the listener is expected to simply pass the salt.

Few people have problems understanding literal meaning, but it can be poor communication to confuse literal meaning with what the speaker intended to convey. In our culture, when someone who seems to be attracted to you asks you to 'Come back for coffee', answering 'No thanks, I don't want any coffee', could be seen as quite insulting and indeed might wreck a developing relationship. When your super-visor asks you 'Would you mind checking these files for me?', then it may be quite cheeky to answer, 'Yes, I would mind, but I am willing to.' 'Would you mind' is often simply the polite form of a command.

Action meanings

The action or illocutionary meaning of an utterance is what it implies or suggests. 'Can you pass the salt' suggests that the listener pass the salt and should not be answered 'Yes'. Similarly, 'It's hot in here', can suggest that someone open a window. People often interpret action meanings without realising it and they can be easy to misinterpret.

In the workplace, problems can arise when people misinterpret action meanings. A famous example from history is when King Henry II exclaimed in anger 'Will no one rid me of this troublesome priest!' Unfortunately, four of his knights interpreted and acted upon this as a request to murder Thomas à Becket, the Archbishop of Canterbury. This caused great scandal and the King maintained that he had simply been annoyed and had been asking a rhetorical question, not expressing a request for action, let alone murder.

A more trivial, but common, example is when an inexperienced secretary interprets the dictaphone recording 'Dear Sir, make the usual apologies', literally and types this into a letter instead of translating it into 'Dear Sir, I regret that . . .'

Connotative meanings

What people say or write often indicates subtle or poetic meanings along with literal and action meaning. Connotative meaning can suggest emotions and feelings, but there is not an exact correspondence between what is said and what it connotes.

Take the following alternative ways of expressing the same thing:
Dear Colleagues

. . . Linda has been fired.
. . . Linda's contract has been terminated.
. . . Linda has left our organisation.
. . . Linda's career objectives are no longer compatible with the needs
     of this organisation.

Each describes the same event, but expresses a subtly different view of it. Take a moment to write down what you think is being expressed by each alternative phrase.

There are no hard and fast rules in interpreting connotative meanings. However, connotation can be remarkably expressive and many speakers, knowingly or unknowingly, disclose many of their feelings in their exact choice of words. 'Mum' often becomes 'Mother' when a child is annoyed. Similarly 'Julie' can become 'Professor Smith' when her secretary is irritated. As well as emotions, connotative meanings can also express how people feel towards things. Someone whose language at work is littered with sporting metaphors is suggesting a particular view of how work should operate – as a competitive game. Someone else may talk of it as warfare, someone else again may use metaphors of construction or growth. Many unskilled communicators mix such metaphors into a hopeless mess!

Connotative meanings can have substantial effects. For example, people may be offended by, or less satisfied with a communication that is brief and suggests that the sender is being brusque. In contrast a brief hand-written reply from somebody senior or famous may suggest personal interest, even if it was actually hand-written in the interests of saving time. It is useful to consider what is being suggested by how something is being said, as well as what is actually being said.

What do the following telephone answering machine messages suggest about Mike Brown? Which would be most appropriate in a business environment and why?

This is extension 4055. Please leave messages for Mike Brown after the tone.

This is Mike Brown. Sorry I cannot take your call at the moment, leave a message after the tone and I'll get back to you.

Hi, it's Mike. I'm not around at the moment, but leave me a message!

The functions of talk

'Language is a subtle medium and it can transmit information of both a semantic and social nature, often simultaneously' (Ellis and McClintock, 1991). Speech enables us to relate to one another. Most speech can be classified under five functions:

* Egocentric utterances
* Questions
* Influencing others
* Conveying information
* Establishing and sustaining relationships

We 'dress' the function of our conversation with a multitude of verbal signals about ourselves. The words we use, our accents, tone, volume, speech errors all give information about us. The use of verbal cues varies according to the person with whom we are conversing. Even more information is yielded by the structure of sentences, the use of repetition, the linking of thoughts and ideas, the variety of words used and the grammatical structure of sentences. For example, most people use different descriptions of products when talking to colleagues and when talking to customers. Interpersonal relationships can be damaged if inappropriate words or sentences are used. Most of us have been 'blinded by science' at one time or another by salespeople. When we bought a mobile phone we ended up buying from the shop that could explain the differences between the different networks and tariffs in a way that we could understand, without patronising us.

Despite the fact that our verbal signals are reinforced or supported by non-verbal ones, often in our day-to-day lives, we are witnesses to communication breakdowns, misinterpretations and blockages. This often happens because the transmitter's attitudes, motives, experiences, language and postures do not link together in a consistent message. Or perhaps the message itself has inaccuracies or the receivers' attitudes, motives and perceptions make them filter the message so that the intended information does not get through. Communication break-downs are the most prevalent symptom of organisational problems.

Often other factors cause communication breakdowns. Most employees do not mean to cause communication problems but often peoples' perceptions of what they are saying and their perceptions of what others are saying are different. A whole chain of communication problems can arise. Some people are better at receiving and inter-preting data than others.

Social meanings of talk

Utterances also suggest things about the relationship between the speaker and the listener. People speak differently to their families and intimate friends, to colleagues whom they see as equals, to people they see as having power over them, or to people that they wish to exert power over. Even when on the surface people are having a serious work conversation, they can at the same time be struggling to prove who is the more powerful, making in-jokes with other group members at the expense of other people present, or flirting.

Forms of speech also indicate the type of social event that is occur-ring. There are many specific ways that this can happen, depending upon exactly what signals are used. For example, most professional talks are prefaced by comments from the chair, who introduces the speaker and their topic. The chair may also explicitly state why the audience is supposed to listen and how the audience is supposed to behave (e.g., 'please keep questions to the end'). Many meetings, ranging from committee meetings, to classes at school, to court sessions, are prefaced by clear signals to show when proceedings begin and end – 'Right, let's make a start . . .' Here, we will be focusing on one important dimension of social events; their formality.

Generally, the more formal the event, the more formal the speech, or perhaps it is the other way around. At the head of department's 'informal' barbecue people can be so inhibited that they all speak very formally; more formally than everyday in the workplace. Sometimes socially skilled people will try to 'break the ice' at events that seem too formal by using more informal speech. Table 2.1 contrasts informal and formal speech. Many social situations are somewhere in the middle.

Table 2.1 Features of formal and informal speech

Informal	Formal
Addressing people informally: by first names or nicknames	Addressing people by title and surname, or position: 'Madam President'
Use of slang, dialect and swearwords	Avoidance of slang and swearwords, minimisation of dialect
Casual use of grammar, not speaking in whole sentences	Careful use of grammatical sentences
Relaxed rules of turn-taking: interruptions, changes in conversation and several people talking at once is allowed	Strict rules of turn-taking, formal requests to speak may even be required. There may be a strict agenda and time limits on speaking. Interruptions and multiple conversations are not allowed
All topics of conversation permitted, including personal topics	Only specified topics permitted, personal topics generally excluded.
Expressions of feeling and emotion permitted	Expressions of feeling and emotion generally discouraged

Communication in formal and informal situations

Most people feel more comfortable in informal situations, but only comfortable being informal with some people such as family, friends and perhaps close colleagues. In a workplace, it is important to maintain the amount of formality appropriate to the particular meeting. Too much formality may hinder a meeting between a salesperson and a customer. Too much informality may hold up a committee meeting and prevent the items on the agenda being covered. The skilled communicator will be able to adapt appropriately to situations at different levels of formality and realise that one can interact with the same people at different levels of formality, depending upon the situation. Some people find it difficult to adjust themselves in these ways. There can be four types of problem:

People who are generally inhibited in formal settings

They may lack confidence in their ability to speak or write formally, be intimidated by the formal setting, find it difficult to articulate their thoughts appropriately, or be afraid of being judged badly by the other people present. None of these problems seems to apply in informal settings, where they will often make more of a contribution. Most readers will have known colleagues who are quiet at work but good fun socially.

People who are generally inhibited in informal settings

Some people can communicate very well when the setting is formal and they understand the rules of that setting, but find the openness and lack of rules in informal settings intimidating. One stereotype is that technical people such as scientists, computer experts and engineers are like this. Our experience is that most people are comfortable in a few informal settings, but less comfortable in informal settings where they know those present less well. With strangers, it can be as difficult to make appropriate small talk as to chair a committee meeting. Most readers will have had colleagues who make a good contribution to work meetings, but are boring on work nights out.

People who tend to communicate informally, even in formal settings

These are often outgoing, uninhibited people who are generally good company. However, they tend to have difficulties restraining themselves and adhering to the rules of formal settings. They may speak or behave inappropriately – for example swearing – or they may hold up business by gossiping, expressing their feelings about everything, talking irrelevantly about topics they happen to be reminded of, or talking about matters that are not appropriate.

People who tend to communicate formally, even in informal settings

These tend to be people who are introverted and inhibited. They may be extremely good communicators in formal settings – for example we know many academics like this – but find it difficult to be unrestrained enough to be informal. In the workplace, they are often regarded as good, efficient colleagues, but not necessarily enjoyable ones.

Assertiveness

Difficulties in communicating effectively in a range of formal and informal settings are often due in part to a lack of assertiveness or confidence. People may be concerned that they will be judged by others and found lacking, hence they either avoid certain types of social situation, or behave inappropriately there. They may also feel anxious in some situations and take this anxiety as further evidence of their lack of appropriate social skills, although anxiety is common in many social situations. Anxiety can lead to excessive self-monitoring, where people think over and evaluate what they are going to say very critically before saying it. This can in turn worsen inappropriate behaviour, as people find themselves saying the very thing that they have worried about not saying, or being unable to think of anything to say that will pass their excessive self-monitoring, or saying something inappropriate.

Anxiety is best dealt with by rehearsing in advance a plan of action for what to say, or how to handle the situation. Remember this requires some thought about how other people may reply. Successfully managing awkward social situations will also tend to increase confidence and assertiveness.

Deliberate manipulation of formality

Given the complexity of the signs by which the level of formality is indicated, further problems can occur when people deliberately manipulate these signs in order to affect other people's communication. The most common manipulation is when people make the situation seem very informal, in order to suggest mutuality and trust, hopefully getting others to disclose confidential information, or act on the manipulator's word. Soft sell sales techniques are of this kind. Unless you happen to know that the other person is always very informal, you should be wary of excessive informality with strangers and acquaintances in the workplace. Perhaps you are being lured into something.

A common sales trick is to ask the customer for a trivial favour, such as a cup of tea, as doing a trivial favour for someone increases the chances of your then doing a larger favour – such as signing the sales contract, they hope. Alternatively, people sometimes suggest unrealistic formality in the hope of intimidating people into agreement or silence. Chairs of some committee meetings try this technique, in the hope of being able to push decisions through the committee. In such meetings, either your view really does not count, in which case you are wasting your time being there, or you are being sold a false view of the meeting by somebody who is trying to control it. The only way of testing this is to challenge the presentation of the meeting as a highly formal one. For example, try asking a question, even though this is being presented as being out of order. Perhaps you will get an answer, perhaps it will encourage others to speak up, or perhaps you will be told not to ask any more questions.

Some people deliberately make their offices seem formal and intimidating; they sit on a high chair behind a desk, visitors sit on a low chair in front of them. Even when you are aware of such tricks, they can inhibit communication. The same can be said of the opposite; if your formal appraisal is held on comfortable chairs over drinks, then you may relax. Perhaps this is good, but there is a risk of relaxing too much.

We do not think that it is a good idea to use these manipulative techniques to control other people. Even if they are sometimes successful, they are liable to backfire when people recognise what you are doing and you are likely to be gossiped about as a manipulator, making it harder to get away with it in the future.

Cultural differences in formality

Another consideration is that there are cultural differences concerning how informal and formal different social situations are expected to be. Some cultures are much more formal in the workplace than Britain and colleagues would generally call each other by their titles and surnames. Cross-cultural differences also exist in how formality and informality are indicated. For example, until recently the French tended to avoid the use of first names until much further into a relationship than would be normal in Britain.

Another interesting cross-cultural example is that in the UK adults tend to show off and be outspoken in formal situations but be more reserved in informal ones. In the USA it tends to be the other way around. Look at MPs' behaviour in the Commons compared to Congress in the USA and you will see this quite clearly. Gregory Bateson, the anthropologist who first described this difference, suggested that it was due to different child-rearing practices: in the USA adults watch children showing off, in the UK children watch adults showing off, although such differences may be eroding. As a result, the British often find Americans remarkably quiet at conferences and seminars, while Americans find the British rather rude and outspoken. Then they go off to meet socially and are puzzled as their colleagues transform into the apparent opposite.

Summary

To sum up, face-to-face communication involves a lot of information from different channels and conveys several sorts of meaning at once.

Meanings include the literal meaning of what is said, action meaning, more subtle connotative meaning and signals about the nature of the social situation. Literal meaning often forms only a small part of the entire message that could be attended to and skilled communicators will be attentive to other types of meaning.

Exercises

SELLING COMMUNICATION SKILLS

Imagine that a colleague is being critical of communication skills techniques. Make up two or three lines that you could use to defend communication skills.

CONNOTATION

Keep some of the junk mail that you receive for this exercise. Choose one kind of junk mail, for instance from different financial institutions, or different shops, or different office suppliers. Compare the packaging, presentation and content of three different pieces of mail. What are the different suppliers trying to suggest about themselves and their relationship with the customer? To what extent do you think their presentations will help sales?

FORMALITY

Using the features in Table 2.1, take one of the meetings you are involved in at work and try to decide how formal or informal it is. Is the level of formality appropriate for the type of meeting it is supposed to be? Are there any 'mixed messages' being sent by people's behaviour – e.g., using everyone's first names, but being very polite? Why do you think this might be?

Recommended reading

Argyle, M. (1983) *The Psychology of Interpersonal Behaviour*, fourth edition, Harmondsworth: Penguin.

Ellis, R. and McClintock, A. (1991) *If You Take My Meaning: Theory into Practice in Human Communication*, London: Edward Arnold.

Fiske, J. (1990) *Introduction to Communication Studies*, second edition, London: Methuen.

3 Non-verbal channels of communication

From looking at the variety of meanings that communication expresses, we turn to looking at how meanings are communicated. This chapter reviews channels of non-verbal communication, while the next chapter will look at specific aspects of verbal communication. In groups there are aspects to non-verbal communication; to be able to read accurately and rapidly other people's non-verbal signals and to be able to consider and control one's own non-verbal presentation of self. We will give only a brief summary here.

Objectives

By the end of the chapter you should:

- Know the different channels of non-verbal communication.
- Appreciate the importance of non-verbal communication for conveying emotional information.
- Appreciate the concept of 'leakage' in communication.
- Have thought about the presentation of self in your workplace.
- Be aware of how to improve non-verbal communication.

When we interact, we transmit a variety of verbal and non-verbal signals to each other. Some of these are intentional, some are not. This relies on four main channels of communication: visual – using the eyes; auditory – using the ears; olfactory – using the nose; and tactile – using the skin. In the workplace most people are restricted to the visual and auditory channels. It is not acceptable behaviour in our society to start sniffing each other closely, or feeling each other all over! Indeed, we often pretend that other people have no smell. The fart at work is usually ignored, and smelly colleagues are rarely told, while complimenting a colleague on their nice smell is liable to be interpreted as a sexual overture. Obviously the more intimate the relationship the more acceptable are olfactory and tactile communications. It also depends on the culture. In countries such as Italy and France tactile channels are more commonly used than in Britain. However, in Britain certain types of tactile communication in our workplace are important and commonly used, for example, shaking hands. With familiarity we will use more tactile communications such as the pat on the arm, back slapping and supportive gestures. Nonetheless, for the most part in an organisation we pick up data about each other through our eyes and ears. Birdwhistell (1970) estimated that only about a third of the social meaning of a conversation is carried by the actual words spoken. The other two thirds is acquired by watching what people do.

The classification of non-verbal communication

There are seven basic types of non-verbal signal, but in natural conversation all are commonly used at once. The seven are:

Proximity

How close together or far apart people stay, as well as how and if they touch each other. Basically, more closeness and touching suggests more intimacy, although different cultures have different rules, with the UK being a relatively distant, untouchy culture. The rules of proximity and touching also vary according to social status. For example, children can be touched in ways that would offend adults – don't try grabbing your colleagues' little feet or patting their heads.

Posture

How people stand, sit or walk. Do they seem tense or relaxed; alert or detached? Who are they oriented towards, or away from. Are they 'closed up' with arms and/or legs crossed, or open? In meetings such cues can suggest how people feel about what is going on.

Body behaviours

What people are doing. Twitching jaw muscles may suggest tension. Fiddling with things may suggest nervousness or boredom; so may doodling. On the other hand some people use these habits as aids to concentration, illustrating the important point that there are very few non-verbal signals that always have exactly the same meaning.

Context, culture and individual differences are important in interpreting them. As we will see shortly, it is also important to realise that people can control and manipulate their non-verbal behaviour.

Facial expressions and gestures

Facial expressions and gestures are used to complement language. Anger, disgust, happiness, sadness and fear/anxiety can be recognised from the same facial expressions in every culture that has been studied, but many expressions and gestures that we take for granted vary. For example head nodding means 'no' in some languages.

Non-verbal communication supports the verbal message in two ways. First, by substituting for speech, as with a head nod, or contradicting it, as when somebody frowns whilst agreeing. Second, by synchronising conversation so that people know when somebody is finishing speaking, when somebody wants to say something, when somebody is listening and so on.

Gaze and eye contact

How people gaze and at who or what also conveys information. When two people are conversing, they orient to each other and usually make eye contact to begin with, then continue to look at each other intermittently as they talk. If they are getting along well then they may also adopt similar postures and move together in a synchronised way as they talk. Too little or too much eye contact can make interactions feel awkward.

Quality of speech

The quality of people's voices, in terms of volume, tone, pitch, clarity, pace and disturbance (pauses, fillers like 'um', 'er', hesitations and stammers), also conveys meaning. Table 3.1 summarises some of the main meanings. However, as with other non-verbal communication there are also substantial individual differences. Somebody who stutters is not always nervous; somebody with a loud voice is not necessarily always confident.

Self-presentation

Finally, how people present themselves in terms of appearance, dress and so on also conveys meaning and we will enlarge on this below.

Table 3.1 Some meanings of variations in speech quality

Volume (soft–moderate–loud)	Tone	Pitch + volume	Pace (fast to slow)	Speech disturbances (pause fillers, stuttering, omissions)
Soft – sadness, affection	Sharp voice – complaining, helpless	High pitch, low volume – submissiveness, grief	Fast speech – anger, surprise, animation	Too many pause fillers – boredom
Moderate – pleasantness, happiness	Flat voice – sickly, depressed	High pitch, high volume – activity or anger	Slow speech – sadness, boredom, disgust	Too few pause fillers – anger or contempt
Loud – dominance, confidence	Breathy voice – anxious	Low pitch, low volume – boredom and sadness		Stuttering – hesitancy, anxiety
	Thin voice – weak, submissive	Low pitch, high volume – dominance		Omissions – anxiety, lack of confidence

Source: Adapted from Niven, 1994: ch. 1.

The functions of non-verbal communication

Non-verbal communication augments verbal communication and can even replace some of it, as when a gesture or a facial expression is used instead of a word. It is also used to synchronise and manage conversation. These functions are important but in the context of group communication we can largely take them for granted. More important perhaps is the emotional information that non-verbal signals convey about how people feel, what sort of people they are and how they get along with us. The impression we form of others is to a great extent based on non-verbal communication. We usually remember the gist of what people say and know how that affected us. We are less good at noticing and recalling the non-verbal material. Instead, we often simply retain the impression formed without understanding its basis. 'He seemed like a nice chap.' Why? Few of us are daft enough to fall for open verbal flattery. Nonetheless we may think the man was nice because he smiled, made good eye contact, leant forward to show us he was listening and so on. He'll get the contract. His rival won't because he spent too much time glancing at his laptop when we were talking, didn't smile at all and had difficulty meeting our eyes. It is a pity that the second man was selling the far superior product.

In groups, discussion would often be held up interminably if everybody had their say on everything that was discussed. We routinely make judgements about how other people feel in groups on the basis of their non-verbal signals. The chair may presume that there is a consensus unless anybody signals unhappiness. A skilled chair will scan all others present and pick up on non-verbal signals that suggest a wish to speak, unhappiness, or uncertainty. Less skilled people in groups can be remarkably insensitive to non-verbal signals, particularly if they are nervous themselves. Most readers will have been subjected at some time to a teacher or colleague making a presentation who continued to talk in a boring, long-winded, incomprehensible or irrelevant manner, oblivious to the non-verbal signals that the audience was bored and restless. We have seen people persist with their presentations despite the audience falling asleep, or leaving.

In short, non-verbal information is invaluable in determining how people feel. This does not mean that it is infallible.

Deception and leakage

Most people are less skilled at deceiving others non-verbally than they are verbally and *leakage* often occurs. Leakage is where people accidentally reveal their true feelings by some non-verbal signal that they have been unable to control. People may be trying to be serious, but be unable to control their giggles. They may verbally agree with what the manager says, but non-verbally send signals of disagreement such as leaning back with arms folded, sighing, or looking angry or sad. There can also be leakage by omission, as when somebody smiles with their mouth, but not their eyes, or when the speech receives a standing ovation, but the audience do not look happy or excited while applauding.

It can be informative to look for signs of leakage. Nonetheless, skilled communicators can suppress leakage entirely and may also 'leak' deliberately. For example in Japanese and other cultures where it is important that people are not made to lose face, people can be reluctant to verbally contradict the speaker. Instead they will agree with them, but show subtle non-verbal signs of unease. Their expectation is that the speaker will detect their unease and propose an alternative course of action that they can agree with. Some staff handle bosses like this in Britain as well. People may also deliberately leak signals about feelings that they are awkward about expressing verbally. In flirtation, people may 'accidentally' touch each other.

It is useful to look for leakage cues as one aspect of non-verbal communication, but it does not provide reliable or accurate information about people's true feelings. With all non-verbal communication, the meaning of the signals is always somewhat ambiguous and while the receiver may be able to work out *what* the transmitter is signalling, this does not tell them *why* the signal is being sent. Yet, without knowing, or guessing, 'why' the message can be difficult to interpret and impossible to act upon. Non-verbal signals often require clarification and, as we will see in the next chapter, the receiver's next step is often to request clarification.[1]

For example, while a group discussion is going on a person may sit withdrawn, looking angry. Among the reasons for this could be that the person is:

- Really angry about what is being discussed.
- Angry about something else that happened before the meeting.
- Pretending to be angry in the hope of getting their own way.
- Annoyed at the current speaker, but for reasons that have nothing to do with the current discussion.
- Daydreaming and actually looking angry about something from their past.
- Someone who happens to look 'angry' when relaxed.

The only hope of discovering which of these is true would be to ask 'John, you seem a bit annoyed?' and see what the response is. Even then, John can lie. Both verbal and non-verbal signals can be sent deceptively.

Dealing with individual differences

People vary considerably in their use of non-verbal communication. We think that there are three relevant dimensions. First, the extent that people are aware of and can control their own non-verbal signals. That is, the extent that they leak information. Perhaps this is a sign of maturity, certainly children leak more than adults. Second, the extent that people are sensitive to the non-verbal signals of other people. Some people are vigilant monitors of other people, other people are less likely to notice their subtle signals. Vigilant monitoring may be related to the personality traits of neuroticism and conscientiousness (see Chapter 5). Third, the extent that people use non-verbal signals when they communicate. This varies from culture to culture and also from person to person. In British or American culture, some people use few gestures, facial expressions, body move-ments or changes in voice quality, others use a lot.

These variations can lead to four sorts of people who may present difficulties for others at work. First, people who transmit very little non-verbal information may be seen as cold, uninterested, uncaring, unlikeable, poor listeners and difficult to understand or get along with. It can be difficult to tell whether they approve or disapprove of anything, and even when they express approval or disapproval, they may be suspected of being insincere because their non-verbal signals do not support their verbal statements. The natural temptation with such people is to treat like with like and to be cold and withdrawn right back. It is usually more successful to exert more communicative effort, by both communicating effectively yourself and trying to read whatever subtle non-verbal signals they do send. Making such effort can 'warm up' such people and make it easier for you to get along with them, even if they remain difficult for others.

Second, people who fail to read non-verbal signals from other people. They may fail to pick up on the mood of meetings, fail to notice how other people are feeling, be unaware of the animosity (or amorousness) of others and may come across as insensitive and thick-skinned. They are not necessarily poor at sending non-verbal signals themselves. Others usually treat colleagues like this with amusement or gentle con-tempt, rather than actively disliking them. They should be dealt with by making sure that your meaning and feelings are conveyed verbally to them, by checking that they have understood, and by encouraging them to observe and interpret non-verbal signals from other people.

Third, people who over-emote and use non-verbal signals so much that they convey extreme or inconsistent meanings to other people. There are substantial cultural variations here. A mundane conversa-tion about the weather in Italian can sound and look like an argument by more muted British norms. Individuals who are extravert and impul-sive may tend to over-emote. In consequence, they can give out strong non-verbal information that can be confusing for others. For example people may take their everyday friendliness for amorousness, or feel confused because the person seems angry one minute and happy the next. At work, they may be seen as hotheaded and irrational. It is important with such people to work out what is normal for them, to seek clarification about how they really feel and to learn the differ-ence between their immediate strong reaction to things and their eventual, more considered feelings on the matter.

The final type of difficult person cannot be described so neatly. Some people use non-verbal communication in a variety of manipulative and awkward ways that can be extremely difficult to deal with. It is not always possible to say whether people do such things deliberately or not, but they will have learned that these techniques are functional for them. Common misuses of non-verbal communication include:

- The speaker who speaks in a slow and steady way, neither giving signals that they are finishing their turn, nor reading the non-verbal signals that others want to speak. Such speakers can be very difficult to interrupt and therefore speak too long. Thus, they always have their say, but at the expense of annoying and frustrating others and seeming boring and pedantic. It may be necessary to interrupt such people.
- The speaker who uses excellent non-verbal communication skills to insincere ends, always seeming positive and encouraging to other people's faces and encouraging them to be open communicators, while giving nothing away themselves. Such people may use the information that they gain by these methods to their advantage later. It is important not to let the pleasantness and effectiveness of communication turn your head away from business issues.
- The speaker who emits subtle non-verbal signals to encourage you to try and draw information out of them. Once you manage to do so, they encourage you to regard your success as evidence of an intimacy between you, which they then use to make demands upon you; 'You're the only one who knows the truth, I couldn't possibly explain to her, couldn't you do it for me?' Some people will try to exploit your active good communication skills by becoming passively dependent upon you.
- The listener who deliberately withholds positive feedback from others in order to get his or her own way. By failing to signal approval non-verbally, they may force others to struggle desperately for their approval, both unbalancing the communication and encouraging others to say, or indeed do, things that they hope the listener will approve of. Do not try and win the approval of such a person.
- The 'passive-aggressive' listener, who never openly challenges anything in group discussions, and may even verbally approve of things, but always discredits this by subtle non-verbal signals. If asked about these, then they invariably deny that they mean anything. There is no point in disputing this. Instead, it can be helpful to point out to them what non-verbal signals they are producing, what they seem to mean to you and what effects they have: 'You say that you don't mean to smirk while I'm speaking. I appreciate that it is a nervous habit, but nonetheless it makes

me feel that you are not taking me seriously and I am likely to become annoyed with you.'

Having good communication skills yourself can help to overcome such difficulties, but it is unrealistic to expect to get along with everybody. It is also unwise to have excessive faith in your own abilities, particularly as some people will exploit your good communication skills if they can.

Self-presentation

The ways in which people present themselves affect how they are perceived and how they communicate with others. Initial impressions of other people are extremely important. Studies of diverse social situations, from job interviews to singles bars, show that people form impressions about other people within a few seconds of meeting them. They then maintain and develop these impressions by seeking further evidence for them during the interaction, rather than forming a balanced opinion about the person on the basis of all the evidence (e.g., Goffman, 1959; Dion *et al.*, 1972; Forgas *et al.*, 1983; Stevenage and Mackay, 1999; Vonk, 1999). This is not what most people believe that they are doing and it may contribute to unconscious sexism and racism, amongst other problems.

The appropriate presentation of self varies depending upon culture, upon the social situation and upon what social role the person is playing. For example, men are expected to wear a suit and tie to a formal job interview in this country, but this is not expected during a meeting with your academic supervisor at university. In some Islamic countries, wearing a tie is seen as being inappropriately 'Western', but nonetheless formal dress would be worn to a job interview. The rules for women are less clear-cut in this country.

The presentation of self involves:

- Clothing, personal grooming and body decoration.
- Personal property.
- The arrangement, design and decoration of one's personal and social space.

Clothing, personal grooming and body decoration

The ways in which people dress say a lot about them. For example, one normal academic self-presentation involves conveying the impression that you are not very interested in clothing – presumably because you have better things on your mind. The 'traditional' university teacher look for men involves a hard-wearing jacket which used to be tweed but nowadays is often some sort of waterproof fabric, a creased pair of trousers and a conventional shirt. Ties are optional. Women may adopt similar dress, but are more likely to vary their clothing. Younger academics may wear a tee shirt, jeans and some sort of jacket.

Even people who protest that they have no interest in clothes, or just dress to please themselves are making a clear statement about themselves in their choice of clothes. It is as well to be aware of and use the possibility of changing clothes to change the impression you convey. Another common excuse for ignoring dress codes is to say that you 'Just want to be yourself'. Is it realistic to see 'yourself' as your clothes? Is it really socially-skilled to insist on this in all situations?

HOW SHOULD YOU DRESS FOR YOUR WORK?

Most workplaces have official or unofficial dress codes. It is usually wise to conform to these. If there is no official code then you can imitate your colleagues, or attend to their, usually 'joking', remarks about your appearance. Wearing jeans in a suit environment, or a suit in a jeans environment are equally likely to draw comment. Another point is to dress for the role that you aspire to. If you want to be promoted then it is unlikely to hold you back if you dress to fit in at that level, by modelling your managers.

A third consideration is how to appear to customers, clients or patients. Other surgeons may appreciate your Mercedes and Armani suiting, but these signs of success will make you seem remote and off-putting to many patients. When you need to communicate easily and openly with people it is helpful to dress more like them. Wise GPs in poor areas do not dress too well, whatever their income.

In most jobs, some ability to vary your dress to fit the situation is useful. We remember the computer support man who always took his jacket and tie off in the car before coming into a university research unit. He looked more natural then lunching with the hairy and bejeaned computer officer.

A final point is to appreciate the difference between 'fitting in' and 'blending in'. Unless you are required to wear a uniform, there is no point in dressing exactly like everyone else and you should be seen to dress well if you can.

What is dressing well at work?   The following suggestions are no more than common sense, but common sense happily ignored by many people, despite the country's increasing love of shopping. You will notice that we are not specifying any particular style.

- Wear clothes that are up to date, but not over fashionable, unless that is part of your work.
- Dark colours are more serious; bright colours more interesting. Choose carefully.
- Wear the most expensive clothes that you can afford. It is better to have a few good outfits than many cheap ones, unless your work ruins clothes quickly.
- Wear clothes that fit. This requires checking your rear view and what happens to your stomach when you sit down.
- Maintain your clothes. If they are dirty or in poor condition it makes a poor impression – including shoes.

Like many defects in communication, it is much easier to spot fashion mistakes in others than in yourself. We do not think that your age, gender or social status exempt you from these suggestions.

Personal property

The things that people own and carry about with them also make statements about them. For example, the quality of the computer on your desk is a status symbol in a university. When we began writing this book carrying a mobile phone and not switching it off during meetings was another common statement about one's importance even if the person 'forgot' to switch it off. By now the mobile phone is commonplace and it is socially unskilled not to switch it off. The type of car a person drives is also a statement. Statements of status are fine, unless they drain resources unreasonably. Does the boss who never actually uses a computer need to spend £3,000 on a new one because everyone else is upgrading to £2,000 machines (that they actually need for work)? Another problem can be that people are prohibited from having things that would aid their work. For example, we knew a telecom engineer who was not allowed to have a 4-wheel-drive vehicle – even though she regularly maintained transmitters on isolated hilltops – because her managers did not have them.

The arrangement, design and decoration of one's personal and social space

If you decorate your office with posters of fluffy rabbits, HIV awareness posters, or lists of computer programming commands and internet addresses, then you are making three very different statements about yourself. Offices where the desk faces the door and the occupant keeps the desk between themselves and visitors invite more formal interactions; offices where the desk faces the window and the occupant turns around to interact with visitors invite less formal interactions.

The kind of workspace you are given also says something about your organisation's view of your relationships with it. Do you work in cubicles, much despised by Dilbert (Adams, 1997), an open-plan environment or in your own office? How does this compare to other people and what does it suggest about your role? To what extent is status in your organisation reflected in a precise allocation of furnishings and office space?

How can non-verbal communication be improved?

The simple answer is by practice, using the following pointers:

- develop skills in observing non-verbal communication;
- interpret non-verbal communication in the context of the total situation;
- beware of the possibility of misinterpretation;
- practice becoming aware of and managing one's own non-verbal communication.

Overall, it is important to recognise that all channels of communication contribute to meaning. It is therefore important both to identify meaning using the full range of information and to be able to use all channels when communicating.

Exercises

Observing non-verbal cues

Choose a specific type of non-verbal cue from those discussed above and practice observing it in other people when they are communicating. Try and work out what they are signalling.

Get two other people to work with you.

Dress for success

As an experiment, try dressing more like the senior staff in your department – don't overdo it or you may look silly or draw attention to yourself. Does dressing this way have any effect on how you interact with them?

You may also like to try 'power dressing': dark, plain colours allegedly make the wearer seem more powerful.

We'd all like to think that we are above such 'tricks', but try them and see . . .

Status in the workplace

Make up a list of the equipment, furniture and other environmental features used in your organisation to show a person's status. Remember that this often occurs even when officially everybody is equal.

Recommended reading

Goffman, E. (1959) *The Presentation of Self in Everyday Life*, Harmondsworth: Pelican.

Knapp, M.L. and Hall, J. (1992) *Nonverbal Communication in Human Interaction*, third edition, Fort Worth, Texas: Harcourt Brace Jovanovich.

Niven, N. (1994) *Health Psychology*, second edition, Edinburgh: Churchill Livingstone; Chapter 1: Interpersonal Skills pp. 3–24; Chapter 3: Communication Process, pp. 43–63.

4 Techniques of verbal communication

Almost everybody already knows some of the basics of verbal communication, so it is not necessary to describe these; readers will be able to say things and understand what others are saying. Instead we will cover briefly a number of methods in verbal communication, including questioning, self-disclosure, dealing with emotion and assertiveness.

Objectives

By the end of this chapter you should:

- Know the different types of question that can be used.
- Understand the basics of listening, attending to and acknowledging emotions and feelings.
- Understand the nature of self-disclosure.
- Understand what assertiveness consists of.

Questioning techniques

Although we use questions every day in our communication with others we do not always do it skilfully. This may therefore block effective communication. Questioning is far harder to study and describe than to acquire and practise (Dillon, 1997).

General points about the use of questions

- The most important part of questioning is listening to the answers.
- Decide your reasons for asking the questions.
- Do not ask too many questions, sometimes they are better rephrased as statements.

- Don't think too much about the next question, when you should be listening to the speaker's answer.

Everybody has encountered people who make conversation by firing a string of questions at you, but seem to have no interest in the answers:

> 'What kind of car do you drive?' 'Do you play golf?' 'Have you any children?'

At the extreme, this kind of approach *prevents* communication rather than facilitating it. The respondent is prevented from saying what he or she really wants and the questioner does not need to make much effort.

Different types of question

Various kinds of question may be used depending on the exact context and what precisely the person asking the question aims to achieve. The most commonly used questions summarised by Niven (1994) are outlined below.

Closed and open questions

CLOSED QUESTIONS

A closed question is one in which there is a restricted number of responses. 'Do you prefer red or white wine?', 'What type of car do you drive?' They are particularly useful for making people feel at ease at the beginning of a conversation. Although one must be careful not to overdo it; too many closed questions may not only seem very unnatural but may also overwhelm respondents making them feel that they are being bombarded with a myriad of questions.

OPEN QUESTIONS

In contrast to the closed question, there are no fixed number of answers with the open question. Instead respondents have much more control in deciding how they choose to answer the question 'How would you describe yourself?' 'What sorts of things have been on your mind recently?' The advantages of the open question are that respondents have more freedom to decide what they want to talk about and it also means that the questioner has more opportunity to take on an active listening role. A disadvantage is that the conversation can wander.

OPEN AND CLOSED QUESTIONS COMBINED

Open and closed questions can be used in combination. This allows the respondent to determine the 'direction' of the conversation. Beginning a conversation with an open question and gradually becoming more specific is very common, e.g., in interview situations or when you do not know someone very well. This method of questioning has been termed 'funnelling' (Kahn and Cannell, 1957).

The 'inverse funnel' is another form of questioning which starts off with specific questions and then moves on to a broader range of topics; the 'tunnel' is yet another kind of sequence which consists of a succession of closed questions. It can become very confusing if a sequence is not provided, mainly because the respondent will be unable to determine what type of question will be asked next. This may hinder communication.

Affective questions

The use of affective questions not only gives respondents the opportunity to consider how they feel about something but it gives the questioner the opportunity to acknowledge the respondent's feelings and emotions. 'How do you feel about my feedback on your paper?' The most significant components of the affective question are concern and understanding. If you are genuinely concerned with people's feelings, then take the time to talk about them properly.

Probing questions

Sometimes people need to be helped or prompted into talking about themselves. Probes and prompts are verbal tactics for encouraging people to do this. They do not have to take the form of a question: 'You seem to be upset, but I'm unclear why.' Such verbal tactics place some demand on the person to provide more details of the situation. Encouraging someone to describe their feelings or behaviour can be extremely beneficial and can help put things into perspective. Needless to say probes and prompts are best used with subtlety.

Leading questions

There are two main types of leading question: conversational lead and pressurised agreement. The conversational lead is when the questioner displays beliefs or feelings he already has, e.g., 'That's great for the company!' or 'I've never seen her performing so well.' Pressurised agreement places direct pressure on people to agree with the person posing the question: 'Aren't computers difficult to use?' Implication is often used in the leading question, which can make the respondent feel obliged to justify his or her views especially if the respondent does not agree with the question, e.g., 'Like all successful managers, wouldn't you agree that a bit of deception is normal?' The responses generated by leading questions are not always accurate and are best avoided. It is perhaps not too surprising that leading questions are commonly used by interviewers in order to provoke disagreement in the interviewee followed by justification of their views.

Questioning can be complicated

As you will now appreciate, questioning is more complicated than it seems at first. If you find yourself asking too many questions then they are probably not the right ones. Perhaps you are talking at cross-purposes and you should allow the other person time to say what they want.

Another tip is that whenever you need to ask people questions for some formal purpose, such as a job interview, or a meeting with a new customer, it is well worth writing out a brief list of questions and trying them out on a couple of colleagues or friends beforehand to see if you get the sort of information that you want. You do not have to stick rigidly to this list during the interview (if the information comes up spontaneously, for example), but it allows you to feel prepared and to know what you want to cover.

The unachievable ideal is that you have to ask just one question, but of course it has to be exactly the right one. To do this, you will need to already know most of the answer and have a good sense of what the speaker is going to reply.

Feelings and listening

Communication is used for conveying information and also for communicating the speaker's emotions. Therefore it is important to learn how to acknowledge and deal with people's feelings during communication.

What are emotions?

Emotions are how people feel. Feelings can be free-floating, that is not attached to any particular object or event, or they can be specifically about an object, an event, or something that has been said. Emotions can be conveyed openly: 'That suggestion makes me angry'. More often, emotions are conveyed by more subtle means. By non-verbal cues alone – the person merely looks angry, but says nothing – or by a mixture of non-verbal cues and veiled verbal cues: the person briefly looks angry, then makes a sarcastic or cheeky comment.

Failing to deal with emotions

A common reason for communication problems is that the listener has failed to deal with the speaker's emotions. This can lead the speaker to:

1   Be dissatisfied with the communication.
2   Avoid further interactions with the listener.
3   Disrupt further efforts at communication by withdrawing, acting insincerely or seeming disruptive.
4   Act in an awkward or non-compliant manner, for example failing to follow the instructions given.

Listeners can fail to acknowledge the speaker's emotions for three basic reasons.

1   They may fail to notice the cues, particularly if these are subtle and/or non-verbal. It is well worth paying close attention to the full spectrum of other people's communications.
2   They may notice the cues, but feel that the emotions are inappropriate, or time-wasting. In fact, acknowledging emotions prevents the interaction being delayed and facilitates openness, which improves communication. This applies both to negative and positive emotions.
3   They may be unable to deal effectively with other people's feelings. They may be afraid of 'a scene' or that they will be expected to do something.

We will next examine how to notice and deal with emotions, in terms of listening effectively.

Effective listening

Many people regard 'communication skills' as a form of public speaking; the more that they can say, the more fluently, the better. Communication also requires listening. People who are 'good listeners' are not merely quiet, but engage in active listening, allowing time for the other person to express themselves. This means waiting when the person pauses and being tolerant of silence while they think, *not* filling every pause with further questions or conversation.

Reinforcing communication is also important. This means showing that you are listening by non-verbal cues such as nodding, smiling and looking at the speaker, using brief verbal cues such as 'um-hmm', 'yes', 'oh dear' and so on. It does *not* involve activities such as staring blankly at the speaker, glancing at one's watch, or interrupting before the speaker is finished. Reinforcing communication also uses reflective listening.

Reflective listening

Reflective listening involves listening to both the content and emotionality of what the speaker is saying, then reflecting both back to them. This is done by briefly summarising what they have said, or how they appear to feel. Some examples are as follows:

Reflecting content

'So, you have been having problems with deliveries this week.'
'You seem to think that this new process will work.'

Reflecting feeling

'You seem quite upset about the problems that you have been having this week.'
'You're quite excited about this new process.'

In the reflection of feeling, the listener will be interpreting both verbal and non-verbal information.

Defusing emotional situations

Most people dislike emotional scenes, particularly if they are on the receiving end of them. This is one of the reasons why people often fail to acknowledge emotions, particularly negative ones: they fear that the situation will worsen. In reality, situations usually worsen when emotions are not expressed and acknowledged. There will either be a scene, or covert hostility or resentment. The reason is that when people get upset in an interaction they may want something done to redress what has upset them, but they also want their feelings to be acknowledged. To be able to vent feelings is important. Indeed, many times there is little that can be done by anyone and nothing that can be done by the listener. Simply acknowledging feelings can help the situation.

Traps in acknowledging feelings

Acknowledging feelings is harder than it sounds. When confronted with someone who is upset, angry or displeased, many people fall into at least one of the following traps:

BECOMING DEFENSIVE

The listener may feel that they are being attacked or blamed and try to justify themselves, or become emotional in return. This will often escalate the scene. Try instead acknowledging feelings without accepting responsibility or blame. Asking if the speaker is really upset with you personally. Allowing the speaker to express their emotions without passing judgement.

For example, instead of saying

'I couldn't help the work being late, I had a lot of other things to do.' (Defensive)

try saying

'I can see that you are annoyed that the work is late.' (Reflective and non-judgemental)

TRYING TO PLACATE INSTEAD OF ACKNOWLEDGING FEELINGS

The listener may try to soothe or calm the speaker, or attempt to 'play-down' or minimise the problem. Specific things to avoid because they often antagonise include:

Saying that you know how they feel (you usually don't).
Producing aphorisms and clichés about how things 'will improve in time', 'look on it as a challenge', and so on. These may be true, but they are no comfort to the speaker at the time.

Saying that other people have it worse than they do. True or not, this does not affect how they feel at the time.
Telling them to compose themselves or pull themselves together. Be assured, that they would if they could.

GETTING UPSET YOURSELF

Upset people can say things that may upset or anger you. If you are not prepared for this, then you may respond emotionally and defensively, escalating the whole situation.

How to acknowledge feelings

Instead try speaking calmly and quietly, continuing to listen reflectively. Acknowledge feelings without falling into any of the traps. Make time for the communication, so that the speaker can calm him or herself down. If you know that a meeting is likely to get emotional, then ensure that it is held in private, with enough time to deal with the matter properly. If an emotional scene starts to develop unexpectedly, then deal with it if the time and privacy is available there and then – get the person out of the corridor into your office for example. Alternatively, cut it short before it gets too emotional, but schedule a meeting to discuss the issues as soon as possible.

PROBLEM-SOLVING IS TO BE AVOIDED

Listeners are often tempted to try and offer solutions to the speaker's problems, or to rearrange their feelings into problems that should be solved. Often the speaker already knows the solution and just wants to express feelings. Often there is no solution, or the speaker will not accept a solution given by you. Often you are not in a position to guarantee that your solution will be effective. Try instead acknowledging feelings, reflecting what the speaker's options seem to be and reflecting what the speaker seems to want to do.

Sometimes at work people will put pressure on others to problem-solve for them. That is, they will try and make the problem 'your problem' rather than 'their problem.' As they 'cannot cope' you have to. Especially if you are the manager, you may be put in situations where it is extremely important to be assertive and explain your limits. For example:

'It is a shame that you have lost your receipts for the London trip, and I'm not surprised that you are annoyed at being £300 out of pocket. I am sorry, but it is against company policy to reimburse you out of petty cash and as you know the finance office require receipts. All I can do is write a letter asking them to reimburse you without receipts, but I am not sure that they will agree.'

Notice how emotions are acknowledged – e.g., 'you are annoyed' – and the speaker describes clearly what she can and cannot do. While this looks simple, consider some of the alternative replies that would be likely to cause problems:

'You know the rules, no receipts, no refund.' (No acknowledgement of feeling.)

'Don't worry, I'll sort this out with finance.' (Pushing the person out of the office and then avoiding them for months.)

'Too bad. I'm not responsible for your stupidity.' (Confrontational.)

'Why don't you just make sure that you claim more next time?' (Problem-solving in an inappropriate (and unethical) manner.)

Manipulative emotionality

Some people have learned to get their own way by making scenes of one sort or another. They are not necessarily doing so 'on purpose'. Emotions used in this fashion include anger, sadness, excessive praise and, perhaps less obviously, general positiveness. For example, children often nag their parents into buying toys by claiming that the toy is the one and only, most wonderful thing ever – only to lose interest in it once they have played with it for a day or so. When emotions are being expressed non-manipulatively, then the speaker will usually calm down once their emotions have been acknowledged and listened to. Signs of manipulation are that the speaker is making explicit demands of the listener and that the expression of emotion is repeated even after it has been acknowledged and listened to at length. When this occurs, it is advisable to state clearly what you are willing and unwilling to do about the speaker's demands. Then stick to your position, despite continued attempts at emotional manipulation. Giving in to emotionally manipulative demands tends to create further such problems in the future, as parents well know.

Self-disclosure

The ability to disclose aspects of oneself can be an effecti\
nication. According to Jourard (1971) disclosing details of oneseir
might encourage others to do likewise thereby facilitating more open
communication. For instance a teacher may say to a student who has
just failed her prelim exams, 'I failed English the first time, but then
I got an A the second time.' This self-disclosure by the teacher may
encourage students to open up more about the specific problems they
are having.

The Johari window

Luft and Ingham (1955) devised the 'Johari window' which incorpo-
rates the idea of overt and covert communication. There are four
aspects of the self covered in the Johari window. The open self is
known both to oneself and to others: everybody knows you are in
love with your spouse. The hidden self is known to oneself, but not
to others: you fantasise about a colleague, but nobody else knows.
The blind self is known to others, but not to oneself: everybody can
see from your behaviour that you are attracted to this colleague, but
you have not yet realised this yourself. The unknown self is not known
to you or anybody else. Nobody is aware that you are attracted to
this colleague because their voice reminds you of your first love.

The purpose of self-disclosure is to increase the open self – what
you and others know about you. You may tell others things about
yourself, and in turn this may lead them to tell you things about you
and about them. This may increase both your open self, and the other
person's open self.

Nature of self-disclosure

Ivey and Authier (1978) list four features of self-disclosure. First, the
use of personal pronouns such as 'I' or 'my', rather than impersonal,
general statements. To say 'Sitting exams can be quite stressful' is not
the same as 'I find sitting exams quite stressful'. Second, to focus on
feelings, rather than facts. Strangers usually begin by talking about
facts, rather than feelings, or by sticking to conventional feelings.
Saying 'I have two boys and I love them to bits', involves little self-
disclosure compared to 'I have two boys, the younger one has a learning
difficulty and that has put great strain on my marriage.' Third, self-
disclosure can be used as a reaction to things other people say; 'My

daughter has a learning difficulty too and it was very hard at first . . .'. Alternatively, people may react to self-disclosure using active listening to encourage further disclosure; 'That must be very difficult for you.' Both are appropriate in different circumstances. Fourth, self-disclosures can be made regarding the past, the present or the future.

Advantages of self-disclosure

Nelson-Jones (1983) lists six positive features of self-disclosure:

1 Providing a model for others. Some people may have rarely practised self-disclosure and not know how to do it or are afraid to do it.
2 Genuineness. It is beneficial to appear a 'real person' and not hide behind a distant, wooden persona.
3 Sharing experiences. To provide others with a new perspective on their situation, which may lead to different ways of managing it.
4 Sharing feelings. This may increase the feelings of caring and understanding.
5 Sharing opinions. This is less revealing than sharing feelings or experiences.
6 Being assertive. Self-disclosure can be used to present your point of view and how you feel about things.

Problems with self-disclosure

However, there can also be problems. Inappropriate self-disclosures lead, first to burdening the other person unnecessarily; second, seeming weak and unstable. Third, dominating the relationship – it being all about the needs of the discloser. Mutual self-disclosure is probably preferable to a one-sided relationship and people whose work involves counselling others – that is, getting them to self-disclose – need to consider how much they are willing to disclose themselves to their clients.

Domination

Domination can occur in the following ways (Nelson-Jones, 1983), all of which involve discrediting the discloser's experiences, in favour of the other person's experiences. 'You think you've got a problem! Let me tell you about mine!' Here, the dominated person is 'not allowed' to have any problems and the relationship may be quite one-sided. 'Let me tell you what to do on the basis of my experience.'

Here, it is assumed that the dominator's experience is somehow more important, valid, or correct, than the discloser's: 'I understand because I had the same problem myself.' Here, it is assumed that the dominator's feelings are somehow more important, valid or correct, than the discloser's: 'I'll take charge and deal with it.' Again, the discloser's experience and feelings are being discredited. Mutual self-disclosure should involve a mutual appreciation of the other person's experience, not an attempt to reconstruct their experience to fit your way of thinking.

Reservations about self-disclosure

People may also be inhibited about self-disclosure because they are afraid of becoming too intense and personal, which may be inappropriate, particularly at work. There also may be concerns about confidentiality: some people find it difficult to reveal personal information to others at all and may fear that others will think less of them. They may also be ashamed to talk about certain topics, such as normal negative feelings. People may also fear facing up to certain aspects of themselves, which they would prefer not to think about too much. They may also be afraid that if they face up to such issues, they may have to change.

Guidelines for appropriate self-disclosure

Whilst there are no set rules on how to self-disclose appropriately, some guidelines can be followed. Nelson-Jones (1983) suggests that self-disclosure should be direct, sensitive, relevant, non-possessive, brief and not occur too frequently. Being direct involves being clear and honest about what you are disclosing, rather than mentioning things in passing, dropping hints or making general comments. Sensitivity and relevance involve working out the appropriateness of what you are disclosing, given the current social situation. Being non-possessive and brief mean not taking over or dominating the conversation, but rather using self-disclosure as a way of facilitating two-way communication. Finally, while occasional self-disclosure improves communication it can easily be overdone and you should not take every opportunity to relate everything to some past experience of yours. This is domineering and can waste other people's time. The aspects of self-disclosure that have been mentioned here merely provide a brief introduction to this topic (see Niven, 1994 for a more detailed coverage of this topic).

Assertiveness

When people feel inhibited about communicating with others, or communicate inappropriately, then this can simply be due to poor communication skills, but it is often caused also by lack of assertiveness. A sign that this may be part of the problem is that the poor communicator is a well-skilled and effective communicator in some settings, but seems inhibited, or overly aggressive, in communicative style in others. For example, some men communicate effectively with men, but have difficulties in communicating effectively with women in the workplace.

What is assertiveness?

It should *not* be confused with aggression, which can actually be caused by lack of assertiveness. Some assertive behaviour can appear quite aggressive, but the key difference is that assertive behaviour considers the rights and feelings of others, even when forceful expressions of feelings are being made. Aggressive responding tends to attack others, assertive responding tends to put forward forcefully the speaker's point of view.

Consider this example:

'Anna, have you got the report for this afternoon's meeting?'
'I'm sorry it is not ready yet.'

(Aggressive response.) 'You stupid woman, I'm going to have to stand up there with nothing to say.'
(Assertive response) 'I'm really annoyed, that means I'm going to have to stand up there with nothing to stay.'

Notice that the assertive response does not blame Anna (it may not be her fault) but does express anger.

Assertiveness involves the following:

- Admitting personal shortcomings (see self-disclosure).
- Giving and receiving compliments: 'That was an interesting talk you gave.'
- Initiating and maintaining interactions.
- Expressing positive feelings: 'I'm really pleased by the way that this work is going.'
- Expressing unpopular or different opinions: 'Now that I've read the sales figures carefully, I don't entirely agree with your interpretation of them.'

- Requesting behaviour changes by other people: 'Next time you want me to lead a seminar for the senior management team, I would prefer more notice.'
- Refusing unreasonable requests: 'I'm sorry, but it will not be possible to write a 5,000 word report by tomorrow. I could manage a two-page outline.'

Two further key features of assertive people may be that they are willing to compromise with other people, rather than always wanting their own way, and that they do not make set assumptions that if they behave in certain ways other people will think badly of them. More assertive people tend to have good self-esteem, compared to passive or aggressive people, because self-esteem and assertion are inter-related.

Assertive behaviour is something that can be learned and assertive people are generally happier and work more effectively. While some people are overall more assertive than others, most people are more assertive in some situations than in others.

Why do so many people find assertive responding difficult?

To cut a long story short, unassertive behaviour tends to be based on fear of the consequences of assertive responding. People are afraid that assertive responding will lead other people to evaluate them negatively as aggressive, as troublemakers and so on. Unassertive responding can be inappropriately passive, or inappropriately aggressive. Table 4.1 contrasts assertive, passive and aggressive responding.

Some people adopt a 'passive-aggressive' style where they are not overtly aggressive, but they will show their aggression via leakage cues and by, for example, 'forgetting' to do work, or doing it poorly in the hope of not being asked again.

Becoming more assertive

Becoming more assertive takes time, effort and practice. It is usually easier to work on specific situations, rather than trying to accomplish general changes.

First, it is necessary to identify a specific situation where you feel that you have problems and describe how you behave in that situation and how others behave. You may work on a particular event, or on a recurring situation. Second, it is necessary to identify specific things that you could do in order to change your behaviour in that situation

Table 4.1 Assertive, passive and aggressive responding

Assertive	Passive	Aggressive
Admitting personal shortcomings	Keeping silent	Boasting
Giving and receiving compliments	Not giving or accepting compliments	Putting down others, while seeking praise
Initiating and maintaining interactions	Not initiating or maintaining interactions	Initiating interactions manipulatively when you want something from others
Expressing positive feelings	Not expressing feelings	Expressing mainly negative feelings
Expressing unpopular or different opinions	Not expressing opinions	Reacting with hostility to opinions that differ from yours
Requesting behaviour changes by other people	Being permissive: letting other people misbehave and exploit you	Getting angry at other people, but without clear explanation or request for change
Refusing unreasonable requests	Agreeing to all requests, but resenting it	Getting angry with the person, not the request

and decide on some changes that you would feel comfortable putting into action. Third, it is necessary to try out these changes and see how they work. Fourth, you may consider further changes. You would usually not want to try to change everything all at once and it is probably not wise to try out your new skills on the most awkward colleague in your department.

Summary

This chapter has looked at questioning, listening and dealing with emotions, self-disclosure and assertiveness, going into some detail about each and offering methods for improving these communication skills. In all cases, it is clear that skilled communication is communication that is flexible and sensitive to the specific situation. It is also communication where you help to create a mutual relationship with other people, rather than a relationship where one dominates or manipulates the other, or where each competes with the other to get their own way. At work mutual relationships can develop and improve with time; avoid communicative strategies that may work in the short term, but will tend to lead to long-term problems – domination, manipulation and competition tend to cause resentment, or avoidance of further communication. As we will see in the next section of the book, social relationships are founded on a sense of mutuality, or intersubjectivity. Our identities and our social groups are both formed intersubjectively and it is to these processes that we will turn in the next two chapters.

Exercises

Open and closed questions

Prepare a series of open and closed questions to find out how a colleague's work is going, then, with their consent, try the questions out on them. Ask the colleague for feedback about how they felt the questions went. Reverse roles.

Practise effective listening

Work with a friend or colleague as a partner. Your task is to listen to them talk for two minutes, about anything that they like, and practise active listening, using only non-verbal cues such as nodding and eye contact. Swap roles, then finally discuss the experience together.

Now practise reflecting, still with a partner. Have them say something, then try and reflect back to them the content of what they said. Also try reflecting the feelings. Get feedback from them about how you did. Swap roles. Repeat the exercise as much as you like.

Dealing with emotion

Make a list of examples of occasions when you have seen other people deal badly with somebody else's emotions. What were the consequences?

Reflecting on assertiveness

Work with at least one other person. Each describe a situation where you did not act assertively, then discuss how you might have acted differently.

Recommended reading

Adler, R.B and Towne, N. (1993) *Looking Out/Looking In*, seventh edition, Fort Worth: Harcourt Brace Jovanovich.

Hargie, O.D.W. (1997) *The Handbook of Communication Skills*, second edition, London: Routledge.

Nelson-Jones, R. (1983) *Practical Counselling Skills*, Eastbourne: Holt Rinehart Winston.

5   Myths of personal identity

Self-improvement is popular: 'Be yourself', 'Be all you can be', 'Follow your vision'. ... But who are you? This chapter looks at personal identity. It will suggest that although it is widely believed that people have stable personal identities, this idea is not very helpful for understanding social relationships. People's identities are formed in social interactions. The idea of a stable personal identity leads to the expectation that communication should be about other people discovering and appreciating your true identity, and you doing likewise to them. Put into practice, this view leads to regular disappointment when you are not appreciated for yourself and when others fail to act 'as they should', that is according to how you had imagined them.

Objectives

By the end of the chapter you should:

- Be aware of five-factor personality theory.
- Know the myths of identity based on a dualist view of mind–body relations.
- Be aware of the practical communication difficulties that can arise from accepting these myths.

Is identity stable?

> All the world's strange except you and me, and even you are a little strange.
>
> Traditional proverb

We tend to think of ourselves and other people as having varied, stable, consistent personal identities that we are able to understand.

To an extent this is a myth. People often behave very differently in different social situations and may change markedly over the course of their lives. Over a lifetime, even a person's appearance may change so much that in some cases it cannot be proven that they are the 'same' person as the younger person that they claim, or deny, that they are – this has come up in some trials for war crimes, for example. Throughout this book, you will see examples of behaviour that are determined largely by the social situation.

Without social interactions, people can find it difficult to sustain a sense of their own identity. People who are completely, or almost completely, isolated, such as religious hermits, kidnap victims and people who live alone and rarely leave the house can experience disorientation and loss of identity. They may dwell on the past, to give themselves a substitute for social contact; become disoriented in the present; focus excessively on even the most minor social contacts, which may be one of the reasons why kidnap and torture victims can become attached to their captors; and may even hallucinate other people or have imaginary conversations.

A stable personal identity is a socially constructed phenomenon that most people internalise and believe in at least to some extent themselves. This stability is not due to something solid and unchanging, but is a stability caused by many different social forces pulling in different directions like ropes holding up a tent. A well erected tent can seem extremely stable, but it can nonetheless change shape or fall down surprisingly easily if even only one rope changes tension or breaks.

This stability can be described in terms of personality traits. Nowadays many personality psychologists favour the 'Big Five' model of personality because many studies have found that people vary along five dimensions of personality that are fairly stable (e.g., McCrae, 1992). As summarised by Zimbardo *et al.* (1995) these dimensions are:

- Extraversion–Intraversion: sociable, warm and positive versus quiet, reserved and shy.
- Agreeableness–Disagreeableness: straightforward, compliant and sympathetic versus quarrelsome, oppositional and unfeeling.
- Conscientious–Uncontentious: achievement–oriented, dutiful and self-disciplined versus frivolous, irresponsible and chaotic.
- Neuroticism–Stability: anxious, depressed and self-conscious versus calm, contented and self-assured.
- Openness to experience – Not open to experience: creative, open-minded and intellectual versus unimaginative, uninterested and narrow-minded.

This taxonomy is very general, broad and primarily descriptive. There have been some attempts to relate aspects of personality to basic biological characteristics that might be inherited or acquired very early in life, but individuals' social situations and their life experiences usually play a large part in what they seem to be like or how they behave. If one wants to describe a person's general, stable character then this taxonomy is the best job that psychology has done to date. It can predict what people are like across a range of situations, but within a *specific* situation other factors, described throughout this book, may be more important.

Even people who are quite extreme on one of these dimensions may behave and think differently in a specific situation and may change across their lifetime. Someone who tends to be highly neurotic may teach themselves, perhaps using therapy or meditation, to become calm, contented and self-assured, at least most of the time. Someone who is naturally agreeable may become highly disagreeable in a social situation where they feel that they are being criticised or challenged in serious ways, for example, if their ability to do their job is questioned. Someone who is naturally introverted may learn to behave in an extraverted manner in order to do their job well, if it involves a lot of contact with other people. For example, students are sometimes surprised when a witty, entertaining and vivid lecturer seems rather shy one-to-one. Someone who is generally agreeable may become disagreeable if their job involves fighting for resources within an organisation against other disagreeable people. Whatever their personalities, people show a complexity and flexibility of response that makes it difficult to capture 'identity' as the simple result of personality traits. While there is some merit in the idea that different personalities will do better in different jobs, the realities of life mean that the 'perfect' character is not often available for every job and that most people's work involves learning and development, rather than slotting into a predetermined role according to their predetermined character.

For these reasons, we are not going to draw heavily on personality theory to discuss identity. Instead we will treat identity as involving how you seem and how you feel in everyday life. A major motive for joining groups is to acquire a sense of our own identity (Tajfel, 1981).

Myths about identity

Much everyday talk about identity, as well as much English language psychology, remains based on Cartesian dualism: people consist of a mind and a body. Your mind is hidden from others and has a consistent nature known only to you. Other people see only the outward work-ings of your body and these are usually valued as somehow less important than your inner mental workings. Your mind is your 'real' or 'true' self. French and German psychology has always been critical of this approach (e.g., Merleau-Ponty, 1962; Tolmin, 1994) and modern social psychology is gradually moving away from it as well (e.g., Sapsford *et al.*, 1998).

If identity is a stable, but hidden, personal characteristic, then it makes sense to see social interactions involving people as trying to infer other people's 'hidden' identities from the limited information that they have available. A common analogy is 'reading' other people; indeed people sometimes suppose that psychologists can 'read' others in some special way. According to this view, a large part of social interactions consists of 'reading' others, while they attempt to control the verbal and non-verbal information that they present for reading in order to present an idealised, usually positive, identity to the world. Of course, both parties in any interaction are doing the same things – reading and presenting – resulting in a kind of game; *The Games People Play* (Berne, 1964). People want both to manage their self-presentations and to be appreciated for their real selves. This is, in our opinion, a flawed view which leads to some unrealistic everyday myths about identity:

- People should see you in the same ways that you want to be seen.
- Your identity is formed by your past life experiences and, as you cannot change these, you are stuck with the identity that you have acquired until better (or worse) things happen.
- It is extremely important that other people think well of you.
- The 'real you' is very different from the social person that other people see.
- First impressions of other people are not, or should not, be that important in deciding what they are like.

Let us look at each of these myths in turn.

People should see you in the same ways that you want to be seen

One of the wisest things that we have ever heard is that it is a mistake to judge other people as if all, or even any, of their behaviours were oriented towards you. Most of us are healthily self-centred, but this leads us to fancy that others think about us, for good or bad.

Realistically, most people think about you as much as you do about them: unless they are in love with you at the time, rather little. Other people are not the supporting actors in a movie where you are the star; they think that they have the starring roles themselves (usually in a movie with a different plot). This itself is the way of the world, not an insult. Yet many people confuse the indifference and thought-lessness of others with deliberate attempts to offend. Or, they look so much to others for praise that they read the slightest signs of positive or negative interest as being important.

It is not other people's responsibility to see you as you would like to be seen. You may be the world's wittiest and wisest person, but few people will bother to ask your opinion if you never open your mouth during meetings. You may well be a tender and sensitive soul who protects yourself by cracking rude jokes and clowning about, but the latter is what other people see and you shouldn't be horrified if you are the butt of insensitive practical jokes during the Christmas party. Nor is it much use protesting that you are not 'really' author-itarian, even if you are forced to lay down the law sometimes as a teacher, because your students will relate to you as an authoritarian. At the extreme, politicians who start wars don't normally see them-selves as genocidal, power-crazed maniacs, although this may well be how the enemy see them. Most wars are started because the politicians feel they have no choice.

Not being appreciated for your 'real self' at work is a common griev-ance, but one that many people accept. Many people do work that they do not find very fulfilling and they would prefer to be judged as a person by other standards. To use an obvious example, in most university towns these days waiting and bar staff include many students who do not see themselves primarily as 'barmen' or 'waitresses', but have got used to customers making incorrect assumptions about the sorts of people who work in catering jobs.

At work, people's identity is often constructed primarily around their specific role in the organisation and changes in role, such as promotion to a more managerial position, can lead to shifts in identity. For example, it is an old cliché that when the union representative gets promoted to management her support for staff concerns will be diluted. Instead of leading the demands for industrial action, she may find herself required to circulate letters threatening people with the sack if they engage in the action, even if she privately continues to support it. In such situations the display and interpretation of identity can become very subtle. The manager may be unable to openly support the strike, but may leak signals that she is in covert support. Or, she may indeed give clear signals that she is not. In such sensitive situations, skilled communication is very important to convey things that cannot be discussed openly.

Leaking identity information

The following are extracts from two different letters circulated to staff in organisations contemplating industrial action. The extracts are based on real examples, but are fictionalised.

> . . . The nationally-agreed offer is above inflation and we remind staff that failure to attend for work is in breach of contract and will be dealt with severely . . .

The message here is firmly 'Don't strike'.

> . . . The nationally-agreed offer is above inflation and we are confident that the erosion of conditions will be resolved in national negotiations. We remind you that days of industrial action are deductible from pay and require that you notify your head of department if you plan to take part in the action so that your pay can be adjusted accordingly. . . .

The message here is, 'We cannot approve of strikes, but you are free to go ahead if you don't mind losing pay and are not too frightened of your head of department.' It also devolves responsibility to departments.

On being questioned by journalists, the heads of both organisations expressed regret at the decision to strike and opposed the strike. In other words, they officially took the same line. The leaked messages are quite different. The first is impersonal and refers to 'staff' in the abstract and passive. The second is personal, using 'you' and is more concrete. The first suggests a firm management controlling staff, the second suggests that everyone is part of the same organisation and should act on their conscience. The two give quite different impressions of the identity of the managers writing the letters.

It can also be problematic when people at work expect to be appreciated and treated mainly according to their role in the managerial structure, rather than according to how they interact with other people. When a manager appears to be unable to make informed decisions, but expects her slightest whim to be enacted, then there is a serious problem. When a secretary prints and distributes documents in which he has spotted a serious mistake, because it is not in his job description to check documents, then that is also a serious problem. In such cases, the people involved often wonder why their colleagues come to dislike them when they were 'only' doing their jobs. Like most other aspects of identity, doing your job is maintained by tensions, here between the demands of the job role, social interactions with colleagues, and maintaining a separate sense of self.

Other people tend to judge you on how you behave and your current social role, not according to what you are like in your own mind. This means that relationships of all kinds, including working relationships, require interpersonal care and attention. If you want others to see hidden aspects of yourself then you must show these to them and if you want to find out what they are like, then you must be willing to listen to the views of others.

You believe your identity is formed by your past life experiences and, as you cannot change these, you are stuck with the identity that you have acquired until better (or worse) things happen

Even young babies have their own personalities and some aspects of personality appear to be quite stable across people's lives (see Robins and Rutter, 1990). Some babies appear to be more socially-skilled than others right from birth. This does not mean that other children cannot be taught social skills. Some babies seem more easygoing than others, again this does not mean that anxious or angry babies are doomed to remain anxious or angry their entire lives.

It is clear that life experiences and personality mould and form each other across a life. Studies of life histories and biography suggest that no set of life events guarantees happiness, or misery. Most lives contain both happy and sad events. Many lives contain real tragedies and frustrations. These alone do not determine how people are. What seems to be important is how people manage and interpret the things that have happened to them. People construct stories to describe and make sense of their lives and in so doing help to set how they see themselves. Such stories are usually part private, partly socially-constructed (McAdams, 1993).

At work, two people with the same jobs, salaries and accomplishments may see themselves and be seen very differently. Perhaps one is a woman who took time out to rear children. She is seen as having done 'very well' and is pleased with what she has accomplished. On return to work she took a relatively junior job and has been promoted quickly. Maybe the other is a man who is rather younger, has been in the job longer and has been passed over for further promotion. He is seen as an OK . . . but . . . sort of employee and is not particularly happy in his work. He thinks that he deserves more and resents the woman for being promoted to his level so quickly. She resents him, because he is younger and 'Could have made more of himself if he didn't spend all his time complaining.'

It can be dangerous to be labelled a failure at work, and often unfair as well. Many successful people have learned how to relabel failure as success. For example, senior executives who manage companies that fail or run into serious problems often go on to even better paid positions with other companies, rather than being considered unemployable. They have learned to sell themselves as being skilled at managing in adverse conditions, rather than as being skilled at making companies bankrupt or vulnerable to hostile take-over. It could even be argued that if a company is doing extremely well, then it may take little skill to manage it.

Again, it should be clear that identity is something that is constructed and that can be reconstructed with thought and skill. In their lives, most people experience things that affect their identities in dramatic ways and most people sometimes feel that they have failed to live up to themselves in some sense. It is important to learn to recognise and appreciate the positive aspects of things along with the negatives. Changes in identity across the life span can go in both directions; we may not fulfil everything that we first intended to, but we may well have other experiences and accomplishments that we never imagined. Or we may easily accomplish the goals we planned for ourselves, to discover that we are bored and stagnant, and so move on to something else.

Depressed people tend to dwell on the bad things that have happened to them and cognitive behaviour therapy theorises that this dwelling on the negative makes depression worse. Finding the positive and being realistic about the negative can be more helpful. A healthy sense of identity is perhaps one that is strong but flexible enough to adapt to your life as it was actually lived, avoiding 'shoulds', as in for example 'Because I am a doctor I should have . . .' and then belittling one's life; 'It is terrible that I am only a GP in a boring little village.' A more positive view would be: 'I thought I would find a cure for cancer, but my life as a GP has been very satisfying and I have discovered that I am less of a scientist and more of a people person than I thought when I went into medicine.' The way that we think about ourselves affects how we feel about ourselves (Dryden, 1996).

Difficulties in adjusting identity – personality disorders

People who have great difficulty in adjusting or changing their identities across the life span are sometimes diagnosed as suffering from
'personality disorders'. These are not the violent crazies that
Hollywood loves, but merely people whose view of themselves and
their relationships with the world is fixed, nearly impossible to change
and involves an unrealistic or dysfunctional view of themselves. The
details of the different personality disorders are not relevant here, but
one feature of several of them is that the person has great difficulties
seeing that their behaviour helped to cause some of the bad things
that happened to them. They may be unable to maintain a relationship or even friendships over a long time period, because in their view
other people always let them down or betray them. They tend to
construct their accounts of events so that they were always in the
right. This makes it impossible for them to learn, for instance, that
being very jealous of your partner may drive them away, even into
someone else's arms. Instead, the eventual affair is taken as evidence
that the jealousy was justified all along. Rather than being less jealous
in the next relationship, they become more jealous, making things
even worse.

It is extremely important that other people think well of you

It is indeed important that *some* other people think well of you. People
need to feel that they belong somewhere and that they have other
people who care about them and provide them with social support.
The most common way that people achieve this is to have a long-
standing intimate sexual relationship with one other person: marriage,
we'd say, if it were not for the falling rates of marriage and rising
rates of 'serial monogamy' and open same-sex intimate relationships.
Other people get similar support from other sources, such as family
and friends. Oddly enough, whoever these close people are they tend
to think well of you even when you ill deserve it, and you may feel
free to misbehave in front of them.

For the rest of the world, it is nice if other people think well of
you, but not extremely important, nor possible, that everyone think
well of you. As already described, most people don't think of you at
all. On those that do, a colleague once said that when addressing an
audience he always assumed that at least one person in the audience
hated him, or what he was saying. This may not be true, but it is a
safer assumption than hoping or expecting that everyone likes you.

It is practically impossible to please everyone and if you try, then you risk pleasing no one. Worse still, if you try always to please whoever you are interacting with at the moment, then you will tend to say and do different things to different people, which can cause a lot of trouble when word gets around.

However, in most workplaces there are some people whom it is important to please as best you can because the troubles that they will cause you if you don't are not worth it. Most readers are probably thinking 'boss' but bosses are not the only people who can wield power at work. How does one please people? Let's look at this question carefully. Do we mean pleasing people all the time? This may be unrealistic and probably requires you to take a short term, superficial view of pleasing. For example, you could lie and say that the report is ready when it is not, but this avoids displeasure now at the risk of worse displeasure later (or an enveloping tissue of lies).

It is appropriate to decide to make some other people's needs and wishes a higher priority than others. Indeed failing to set such priorities can lead to stress and difficulties as you may fail to manage all the demands that everyone is making on you. As we saw in Chapter 3 on assertiveness, this does not mean simply 'pleasing' people all the time. If you form a cohesive group at work, then you are likely to try to meet the group's needs as well as your own.

The 'real you' is very different from the social person that other people see

Everybody has private thoughts and feelings that differ from those they express publicly, and everybody behaves differently in different social situations. Most people have some private thoughts and feelings that are 'worse' than they would express in public, and some that are 'better'. Everybody also has more access to and interest in their own lives and feelings than they do to other people's. In this sense, you are bound to know more about yourself than other people do.

This does not necessarily mean that you know yourself 'better' than other people do, or that you can always have the last word concerning what you are like. People commonly have distorted and incorrect opinions about themselves. For example, most people surveyed believe that they are 'better than average' drivers, which is of course impossible as the average represents the middle and at least half the people must be worse drivers than average. All those better than average drivers are happy to criticise other people's driving habits. In a nutshell, people tend to regard bad aspects of themselves as being forced on them by the situation, but regard good aspects as being due to their 'real' nature. They tend not to extend this kindness to other people, whom they tend to regard as behaving, well or badly, because of their nature. 'When I take risks overtaking it is because I am in a hurry to get somewhere important; when other people do it they are reckless maniacs who needlessly endanger my life.'

In understanding yourself at work it is extremely useful to listen to and consider feedback – in all forms, including non-verbal behaviours – from colleagues. There will be more on this in the next chapter. For now, consider that perhaps if your passengers are often nervous, this may be due to your poor driving, not to their nervous dispositions. You will appreciate that many people can be remarkably insensitive to feedback about certain aspects of themselves.

First impressions of other people are not, or should not, be that important in deciding what they are like

Let's concede the moral point here: people should not judge other people too hastily on superficialities such as their appearance, age, gender, race or current social role. Unfortunately, we do not have the time to get to know everybody that we interact with so such judgements are common and probably inescapable. Like it or not, numerous studies show that first impressions count massively in virtually all social encounters. Such impressions are formed within as little as a few seconds of meeting another person. As we describe in Chapter 3, once impressions are formed, people then tend to seek evidence that confirms the initial impression. It is difficult to recover from a bad first impression, but possible to damage a good one.

We all like to think that we can resist such superficial judgements. The research evidence is that we cannot, and that knowledge and training do not eliminate superficial judgements. The best that one can do is to appreciate these biases in yourself, and also to resist setting up new social encounters at work in a way that encourages first impressions to dominate.

Various sorts of expert know that most people make superficial judgements, but kid themselves that they are immune from this. These include counsellors who think that they can 'really' get through to people, personnel officers who think that their job interviews are unbiased, communication psychologists who offer simplistic schemes for reading body language and streetwise folk who think that they can always see right through people. In fact everyone can be conned by someone who is willing to put sufficient effort into it and in confidence tricks it is common that the trickster convinces the victim that he or she is getting the better of the trickster or somebody else. Below the level of criminal behaviour, manipulative people can play games such as presenting themselves one way, but allowing the other person to easily uncover their 'real' nature. For example, they may let the other person 'discover' they are upset, which commits them to doing something about it that they might have resisted if the upset had been explicit from the start. For sincere and non-manipulative people, it is generally a good idea to make as good an immediate impression as possible. That alone may not get you far, but it can take a lot of work to overcome a bad first impression.

Sales, in the broadest sense of the word, often capitalises on the power of first impressions. Cynically, it may be hoped that a friendly waiter, charming sales executive, charismatic business consultant, or even soothing telephone call-queuing message, will cause the customer to overlook the mediocrity of the product, whether that is indifferent food or banal business advice. Sadly, even the world's best product can fail to sell if the sales staff do not make a good first impression.

For example, businesses often choose computer software on the basis of what the sellers say that it can do. This requires sales staff to be able to describe complex technical functions in language that managers can understand and relate to. Some software sellers are better at selling than at implementing and supporting software, but even excellent software still needs to be sold.

When being sold something, it is wise to be wary of first impressions, but when selling it is wise to create a positive first impression.

Summary of the identity myths

In short, identity is not a fixed thing but a flexible one that varies from situation to situation. A person's identity is worked out during interactions with others and thus can and does change. However, people tend to appreciate that their behaviour is often governed by the situation, but fail to extend this to other people's behaviour, which they attribute to their nature. In the next chapter we will look at how identity is socially-formed.

Leadership as a myth: a special case

Leadership is regarded as an important aspect of a person's identity at work. It is interesting that research on leadership has shifted over the years from a study of the stable personality characteristics that

define a 'good' leader to the study of the workplace situations that
enable different styles of leadership (McKenna, 1998: Chapter 8).
Earlier studies of personality characteristics failed to discover a consistent personality that made for good leadership and situational factors
are now seen as much more important. Aspects of leadership, such as
'charisma' are no longer regarded as being stable personal characteristics of the leader, but instead as being the product of the leader's
nature, combined with the business conditions under which he or she
leads and the social environment of the workplace. If there is something unique and special about great leaders, then this may in large
part be due to the attributions of their followers. Furthermore, great
leaders may be lucky. Others with exactly the same qualities are not
accorded 'greatness' for the simple reason that their ideas and plans
were unsuccessful.

From the social identity perspective that we are developing here,
we suggest that the difference between a 'mere' manager and a leader
will often be situationally-determined and, reversing the myths of
identity discussed in this chapter, leaders will tend to be:

- In a position to impose their view of things on other people, whether
  by luck, force of character or an advantageous social situation.
- Willing and able to reconstruct the past – for example trans-
  forming failures into learning experiences.
- Insensitive to the criticisms of others.
- But motivated by the regard of others.
- Capable of making a highly positive, or striking, first impression.

These tendencies are not merely a product of the person. For example,
hereditary monarchs in their heyday could issue orders by divine right
in order to impose their view, rewrite history, ignore the views
of commoners, but demand the flattery of courtiers, and competed
with each other in their palaces and other adornments to make the
wealthiest and most imposing first impression possible. With these
socially-constructed advantages, even fools were sometimes monarchs.

Conclusions

In this chapter we have questioned the idea that people have a stable
identity, looked at some of the difficulties that assuming a stable
identity can create and suggested instead that personal identity is
intersubjectively negotiated. The positive aspects of this approach are
that it provides people with the potential to change, avoids seeing

communication as a sort of guessing game, where I try to guess your true nature and you try to guess mine, and, lastly, prevents people blaming the 'other' for not appreciating them properly. In the next chapter we will look at how personal identity is constructed.

Exercise

Describing yourself and others

Write down a series of sentences that describe you. Begin each one 'I am. . . .' Now pick two contrasting people in your life, for example you might choose someone you work with and your partner. Write down a series of sentences that describe each of them. Begin each sentence 'So and so is. . . .'

Look at the sentences. Have you used the same sorts of words to describe these different people? Do the characteristics that you have described for them fit you too?

Finally, write down another series of sentences that describe you, when you are with the people you have described. Begin each one 'When I am with so and so I am . . .' Are there differences between these descriptions and the ones that you wrote to start with? Are these differences due to being with different people?

Work in pairs if you can. Once you have done all of the above alone, look together at the kinds of descriptions that you have used for yourself and for other people. Do you both use the same sorts of description, or are they very different?

Recommended reading

Berne, E. (1964) *Games People Play: The Psychology of Human Relationships*, London: Penguin.

Jenkins, R. (1996) *Social Identity*, London: Routledge.

McAdams, D.P. (1993) *Stories We Live By. Personal Myths and the Making of the Self*, New York: Morrow.

McKenna, E. (1998) *Business Psychology and Organisational Behaviour*, Hove, East Sussex: Psychology Press.

Tajfel, H. (1981) *Human Groups and Social Categories*, Cambridge: Cambridge University Press.

6 The social construction of identity

Objectives

By the end of this chapter you should understand the six basic ideas about identity that are listed below.

Basic ideas about identity

We will draw upon both psychology and sociology and offer you six basic ideas:

1 Identity is fluid, dynamic and negotiable.
2 Identity is communicative. We signify our social identities to other people, interpret feedback from them about what we are like and may modify our identities on the basis of that feedback.
3 Our stable personal identities are constructed to make sense of what has happened to us and how we have related to other people.
4 People's identity constructs are usually socially functional for them, and this can apply even to deviant, damaged or spoiled identities.
5 Identity involves identification with specific groups of people, but also contribution to the nature of those groups; this is a fundamental aspect of social activity.
6 People routinely adopt different identities in different social groups; hence the idea of a social role.

The last two points will be covered in detail in other chapters. It follows from these key points that although you are often defined by your interactions with others, you can also change yourself and how others see you. Furthermore, this is easier to accomplish if you have good communication skills and awareness of how social processes work.

To a certain extent it is possible to adjust your identity by managing how others perceive and judge you, although this does not mean that you should be manipulative about it. Indeed, people tend to disapprove of others who are overly concerned to present whatever identity seems the most socially convenient at the time.

Identity is fluid, dynamic and negotiable

As we will see in Chapter 10, people are strongly influenced by their current social roles and tend to behave and think in different ways according to which role they are playing. Jenkins (1996) emphasises that individual identities are complex and governed by the ways that the person interacts with others. Identity is a product of these interactions. Some people have quite straightforward identities because they tend to play a limited number of social roles and interact only with certain kinds of people. Others have complicated identities, even confusing ones, because their roles and interactions are diverse and change over the course of their lives.

Take, for instance, the use of more or less formal speech and local dialect, as discussed in Chapter 2. A child who has migrated from one part of the country to another – say from Yorkshire to Scotland – may speak with their friends in a Scottish accent, to their parents with a Yorkshire accent and to teachers in received English.[1] They will probably swear with their friends, but not with their parents or teachers. When they go back to visit grandparents in Yorkshire, then everybody there thinks they have a strong Scottish accent. Thus, the child will seem more or less 'Scottish' depending on whom they are communicating with. Although the child can vary pronunciation and vocabulary to suit the social situation, this probably does not happen consciously and there are limits on how much he or she can vary. The dualist view of self, that we are critical of, suggests that somewhere in this variation is the child's 'real' identity and the other presentations are socially convenient façades. This type of view is promoted by people, such as nationalists, who criticise people who do not always speak with a broad Scottish accent. They say that these people are false or not being themselves. Actually, the people are being themselves, but this happens not to fit nationalist ideals of proper Scottish accents. One can be Scottish but speak one of a whole range of Scottish accents and dialects.

In Britain, there are commonly similar class problems. In most regions local working-class accents are seen as 'stronger' than middle-class ones and they usually deviate more from received English.

Educated working-class people face a dilemma. If their accent shifts too far away from their roots then they are criticised for being fake and stuck up. If they retain their dialect then they may be criticised for being 'common as muck', 'hard as nails' and so on. Most people try to cope with such difficulties by varying the extent to which they use dialect depending on the occasion. This is not just a function of one's circle, because everyone else tends to be in the same dilemma. In a formal business meeting people will tend to speak formally, even if they all originally spoke the same strong dialect. Watching football in the pub later, they may all try to speak dialect as best they can, even if they did not learn the dialect from the cradle. The use of language is monitored and socially controlled in most situations. People will criticise others for swearing during a business meeting, but for not swearing while watching football. At the same time, most people feel that there are important boundaries for them, which represent aspects of their identity that they will not change. Scottish people are usually willing to speak intelligibly to other English speakers, but unwilling to take elocution lessons to lose their Scottishness entirely.

There are also more serious problems of a similar kind, as when there are sectarian, racial or other tensions that may make it prudent to present oneself in different ways to different people in order to avoid trouble, or even violence. Situations come up in Belfast or Glasgow, particularly for young men, where it is a good skill to be able to judge which football team you should pretend to support. Most people will be flexible and pragmatic about many aspects of their identity, but will also insist on setting boundaries. Some fervent Glasgow Celtic supporters may be proud to get beaten up, rather than deny their team.

Every aspect of behaviour is socially negotiated in this way. Take dress codes as another example. Most workplaces have a dress code, even if it is never formally stated. Many businesses expect men to wear dark suits, and other clothing will draw comment. Comments will usually be humorous, but nonetheless they will tend to govern behaviour. University staff who are not senior managers usually do not wear suits. Wearing a suit will also draw comment: 'Going for a job interview?' Again, the way that one presents oneself is socially managed. In most workplaces you are technically free to violate the informal dress code, but at the expense of making your deviant clothing part of your identity. In medical schools, medics believe that you can spot the social scientists by their woolly jumpers. In reality, medical school does indeed include medics in blue suits and social scientists in woolly jumpers, but it also includes medics in woolly jumpers presenting themselves as more like social scientists and social scientists in blue suits presenting themselves as more like medics.

It is not so easy to give clear examples, but more fundamental aspects of your identity at work are also negotiated, including the form and content of the contribution that you are expected to make. Staff most commonly feel frustrated because the contribution that they are expected or allowed to make undervalues and de-skills them. For example, many people now work using computer-based forms that determine the information that they should gather from customers and what the outcome should be. When an individual customer does not fit the form, then they have to refer the case to a supervisor. Given major limitations like this that occur in many jobs, it is not surprising that most people feel that their personality is 'more than their work'. They may emphasise their other interests outside work, or their family life, even though they spend most of their lives at work or asleep.

In general, because identity is fluid, most people's identities contain some tensions and contradictions that can lead to change, as well as some clear boundaries. People often use clothing and body adornments to signify their boundaries. The subtle body piercing or tattoo along with the business suit is making a statement about being willing to conform, but only so far. The cartoon socks or tie is making a similar gesture suggesting that you are not just the serious fellow the suit implies. When a formal business uniform is not required, then a whole complex range of clothing styles are available to show 'who you are' and many people put a lot of time and effort into choosing just the right look for them. Most people's aims seem simultaneously to be to look like an individual and to look like whichever group they identify with. This is another reason for the popularity of personal touches such as cartoon ties to adorn the standard business suit.

Identity is communicative

We signify our social identities to other people, interpret feedback from them about what we are like and may modify our identities on the basis of it. Feedback is thus a key concept in the study of communication. If you behave in certain ways towards others, then this affects their judgements about you and how they respond to you. This in turn affects how you will behave towards them in the future. For example, comedians often report that they began making jokes in school to be liked and to draw attention away from some other aspect of their identity that they disliked, be that ethnicity, obesity, perceived unattractiveness or poor school performance. Once regarded as the 'comedian' other people expect the person to be funny and may even laugh when the person is not being deliberately funny. Many people try to be the comedian and fail, perhaps many others are capable of adopting this role, but have no wish to. Acting the comedian requires that the person finds it socially rewarding to make people laugh, is able to make people laugh, and that people do actually reinforce this behaviour.

At work, you are likely to behave in whatever ways other people encourage and avoid doing things that are disapproved of. That is assuming that you are sensitive to feedback from others. Most people's identities require a tension between being socially approved and behaving as they wish. Another way of looking at this is as a tension between your social roles and your personal identity. More is known about social roles than about the stable aspects of personal identity.

In postmodern, global times and, in more affluent societies people are increasingly free to choose how they live and how they present themselves without conforming entirely to historical or local precedents. It remains surprising how in Europe people still adhere to their local cultures (Castells, 1996), but more noticeable is the extent to which people have become freer to adopt and display diverse lifestyles. These often draw upon different elements that in traditional terms are contradictory. For example, distinctions between rural and urban life have largely eroded, but many people are nonetheless attracted to a 'traditional rural life'. In its postmodern form, this life involves such amenities as fitted kitchens of a particular wooden appearance, but which are hardly traditional; living in a 'cottage' that has been enlarged to modern standards and contains an ensuite bathroom; spending an hour or even much more each day in a large car driving on modern roads; shopping in a large supermarket. It is possible to have most of this without living in the country at all.

In most workplaces, staff are neither free to present themselves however they like, nor completely constrained by uniform policies. There are often requirements that, as representatives of the organisation, they should have a specific appearance and follow guidelines in dealing with customers or clients. Many modern organisations themselves have explicit identities upon which such guidelines are based. Such identities have been developed precisely because they can be important in determining the success of a business.

Social identity theory (Tajfel, 1981) furthermore proposes that establishing and maintaining identity is a major motive for joining social groups in the first place. Taking this further, Turner (1987) proposes that becoming a group member involves some simplification and stereotyping of oneself. Over the years, you become more like your workgroup's stereotype. When somebody is a member of only one or two groups and stays a member for a long time, then their membership may become a very large component of their identity. People say 'He lives for his job' and people identified like this often find major transitions such as retirement or unemployment very threatening to the stability of their identity. Some even contemplate suicide. Using the tent metaphor from Chapter 5, if the only large rope holding up your identity tent breaks then your identity will become unstable and need replacement ropes to hold it in place. One of the greatest difficulties faced by the long-term unemployed, particularly men, is what to hold up their identities with. 'What do you do?' middle-class people ask when socialising. If you neither work, regard yourself as a homemaker, nor have a single main interest in life, then you need to come up with something. It has become more common to support yourself on many small ropes (Castells, 1996), but this is harder to describe.

Our stable personal identities are constructed to make sense of what happens to us and how we have related to other people

Identity *is* narrative, rather than being a set of personality traits, or being a list of accomplishments or social roles and responsibilities. The stories that people tell about themselves are used to define how they see themselves and to show others how they would like to be seen. In such stories people construct personal myths (McAdams, 1993). The truth of such myths is irrelevant, people use them to make sense of their lives and themselves. One aspect of these myths is the tone of the story. Most people see their lives as somewhat more positive than is realistic – and they also tend to think that they are cleverer and more attractive than they really are. Different tones are used to different extents by different people. Some describe their lives as comedy, as about the pursuit of happiness, some as romance, which is fundamentally about triumph over life's challenges. Others see their lives in tragic terms – where things go wrong and happiness is fleeting. Also somewhat negative, some use an ironic account where most of what happens to us is incomprehensible and we must muddle along. These life narratives are peopled by what McAdams (1993) calls 'Imagos', which are characters that represent a person's ideals and aspirations (and are quite similar to Jungian archetypes). For example, a university professor might in part characterise herself as 'The Sage' and focus her life story around events where her cleverness and wisdom allowed her to overcome problems and achieve things.

People often see their life stories as 'truth' but of course they are biased, almost fictional, in two main ways. First, any life history is inevitably selective and will only report some events. The choice of events reflects the person's sense of identity. For example, do they focus on negative events where they were treated badly, or on events where they came out on top of the situation? Do they tend to focus on funny things that happened, or on disasters?

Second, most events could be recounted in a number of different ways, depending on the person's view of themselves. Even common major life events can be described very differently by different people. Take coping with a new baby. According to some people this is comedy – things go wrong in humorous ways but you find great happiness. According to others it is tragedy – your life is changed for the worse and you encounter great difficulties. You could also construct romantic and ironic accounts of this event.

The stories that people tell about others also reflect identity, this time more in terms of who is similar and who is different, often described in terms of what is normal, admirable or correct, contrasted with what is unusual, disapproved of, or inappropriate.

For example, there was a research psychologist who was notorious for his uninhibited behaviour during seminars and meetings. He would pull faces if he did not agree with the speaker, ask questions in abrupt and rude ways and one time even began to make hand shadows across the speaker's slide show because it was difficult to read the print on the slides. This man became well known and often discussed, usually with amusement. Why? One explanation would be that his behaviour exemplified the inappropriate, unusual and disapproved within academic psychology, where most people tend to be reserved, serious and polite, at least in formal settings.

Social groups probably also construct accounts of themselves and it seems likely that different groups may choose different styles of narrative, populated by different characters. In one workplace everything can be construed as 'a great laugh', while in another everything is a disaster to be overcome.

Once a person's (or perhaps a group's) identity narrative is well developed, it will tend to be used to deal with new information obtained during social interactions, drawing upon two well-established cognitive processes – assimilation and accommodation. Assimilation is the tendency to make sense of the new in terms of the old. For example, people who see their lives in tragic terms may assimilate even very positive events into their tragic narrative. If they receive a promotion, they will construct this as long-overdue, less than what they deserve and something that could have occurred earlier if only their lives had gone better. In contrast, a romantic might describe the promotion as the deserved outcome of much personal effort and struggle. People with stable identities will tend to assimilate most new information. A stable identity can be a strong identity, but it can also lead to resistance to change. As described in Chapter 4, the extremes of this are the personality disorders. It is also worth mentioning that, as described in Chapter 3, people tend rather quickly to form a view of other people then assimilate new information to it, making bad first impressions difficult to change.

Accommodation is the tendency to allow the new to modify the old. For example, a promotion might lead somebody to revise his or her view of themselves as lacking in ability. McAdams (1993) describes how many life stories include events that are described as being of major formative influence. These include events that led to change, that is, accommodation. People with more fluid identities will tend to accommodate most new information. This can produce a flexible and adaptable identity, but at the cost of having a less strong or clear-cut view of self. At the extreme, Buddhists strive to lose self-identity entirely, for they view it as a harmful illusion. Most people however appear to have a strong need to develop and maintain a coherent identity that makes sense of their lives. Psychoanalysis can be seen as serving this need. Following Lacan (1979), some current thinking on psychoanalysis regards it less as the uncovering of past events or unconscious structures that are 'true' and more as the deconstruction of the client's account of self and life followed by a reconstruction that they can accept and live with.

People's identity constructs are usually socially functional for them, and this can apply even to deviant, damaged or spoiled identities

It is obvious that socially valued roles, such as being a doctor, lawyer or successful manager, are socially functional. So it also makes sense that people promote and take such roles and make them central parts of their identities. Indeed, this has been so accepted that social scientists have hardly studied such conventional and acceptable roles.

There has been much more interest in identities that are deviant, socially unacceptable, unworthy or 'spoiled' to use Goffman's (1963) term. Goffman (1959) developed the idea of identity as a set of social roles or presentations of self, but had little to say about how and if there is a stable self underlying different social roles. However, his major work involved people who had a major dominating social role that could virtually be their identity, such as psychiatric patients and people with disabilities. Other people may have a number of less dominating roles and more ability to shift from one to another. Moreover Goffman himself (1968) emphasised that people could 'step out' of their dominant role, much as actors cease to act going backstage. He documented how mental patients and their nurses engaged in some activities where the roles of patient and nurse were weakened or dropped. Nonetheless, he showed that people can 'become' their dominant social role. This process is never absolute and the cliché that there is more to someone than meets the eye seems almost always true. For example, Hitler was apparently kindly towards children and dogs, when he was not dictating orders about the conquering of Europe and the extermination of non-Aryans. Nonetheless, the surprise is not that people are more than their dominant roles, but that people will adopt unacceptable roles. Hitler is not an example here; he seemingly relished being a dictator.

If we can understand how and why people should identify with a role that is socially unacceptable, then this will inform how identity is formed. The most promising explanation comes from social learning theory (Bandura, 1977). In general, social learning theory proposes that people behave in the ways that they do because they learn that those behaviours are socially functional: people get something out of the role to the extent that they come to identify with it. Among the dominant roles that have been most studied are the institutionalised role and the alcoholic role. We will look briefly at each before turning to less desirable roles in the workplace.

When a person has spent a long time in a total institution (one which controls all aspects of one's life), such as a residential psychiatric hospital, or a prison, then they tend to become institutionalised. They learn ways of socially interacting that are functional within the institution, but can be dysfunctional outside it. In hospitals and prisons, people learn to be passive and to accept decisions forced on them by others. Trying to be assertive and take control only causes trouble, so they learn to avoid it. This can make it hard for institutionalised people to cope outside. Indeed some prisoners deliberately commit further crimes on release in order to return to prison, where they can cope.

Institutionalisation is a dramatic illustration of the tendency for roles to determine identity and behaviour by limiting and controlling the options that people have. The alcoholic role is interesting because it also limits and controls the options that the families and friends of the alcoholic have. As somebody comes to drink more heavily, they will tend to come to associate more with people who tolerate heavy drinking and its consequences, and less with people who do not. They will also learn to conceal the extent of their drinking. Among the people who can become tolerant of heavy drinking can be the alcoholic's family. They learn ways of coping with the heavy drinking, ways of concealing it from the outside world and ways of minimising and managing the problem. It also often affects how the family can interact with others. For example, children may avoid bringing friends home for fear of the drunken condition that their parent may be in. The dilemma is that in finding ways of managing alcoholism, the drinker and the family all risk facilitating the alcoholism. For example, other family members may take over the alcoholic's responsibilities. This, in turn, makes it possible for the alcoholic to be drunk even more often, which makes the family take over even more.[2] Such social processes constitute a 'positive feedback loop' where the fact that things are getting worse tends itself to make things even worse.

To put it rather simplistically, it becomes the family's role to cope with the alcoholic, and the alcoholic's role is to be the problem. When an alcoholic reforms, then this can disrupt the family. For instance the spouse may be used to paying all the bills, choosing the furnishings and making all the domestic decisions without consulting the drunk. Sober, the ex-alcoholic now expects to have a say in decisions, which can cause conflict. The children of alcoholic parents may become independent early and care for their younger siblings. If the parent gets sober, then the children may find their independence eroded. For these sorts of reasons, sobriety may be a mixed blessing and there may be some social pressures for relapse to occur.

In workplaces the same sorts of process occur in a milder form. For example, secretaries, particularly older ones, are sometimes criticised for being passive, demotivated and unintelligent. Are the characteristics the result of social learning? Perhaps secretaries often learn to be passive because they have often been reprimanded for taking the initiative in the past. They are not supposed to take the initiative unless it happens to coincide with the boss's ideas, in which case the boss is likely to get the credit. Perhaps secretaries are demotivated because they may be paid much less than some other staff, but may work just as hard and do work that seems just as demanding. Perhaps secretaries learn to act stupid because if they seem intelligent then they are more likely to be given more work than they are to be promoted. If a secretary comes to act as passive, demotivated and unintelligent, then this will in turn affect what others expect of them. People will tend to give them only simple tasks and not trust them with too much autonomy or responsibility. This results in another positive feedback loop where how the person is treated worsens how they behave, which in turn worsens how they are treated.

Such processes have not been much studied in the workplace, but they are clearly documented in the arena of interpersonal relationships. A person in a relationship where they are told overtly and covertly that they are stupid, passive and worthless will come to believe it and act accordingly. This can explain why people remain in abusive or dysfunctional relationships (see Buchanan, 1996). We can assume that the same applies in the workplace and helps explain dysfunctional behaviour such as that of the secretary described above.

At work, other examples of seemingly dysfunctional identities include the rude and aggressive person whose justification is that 'It's the only way to get people to do any work around here'; the incompetent, who has learned that if you make a mess of things then you get less work, which is fine if you've given up on promotion prospects; and the control freak, who takes over every job because 'If you want a job doing, do it yourself.' The control freak asserts superiority over others, at the expense of having to do their work.

Identity involves identification with specific groups of people, but also contribution to the nature of these groups; this is a fundamental aspect of social activity

Most of this book is concerned with how groups work. Although the material is not specifically concerned with personal identity, much of it will show how individuals work together in groups, how groups change individuals and how individuals change groups. When we describe this as 'fundamental' we mean that this is the very basis of how human society works. Human culture means that an individual person can join a group, bringing along new ideas, words, technologies or merely new fashions that the group will learn, may adopt and often will change to suit themselves. The incomer will also learn the group's existing ways and will adopt them, again modifying them in the process. To use just two examples, it has become common in Britain for people not raised with Christian traditions to send Christmas cards, but they normally choose ones without overt religious imagery. At the same time, the most popular restaurant meal in Britain is now curry, which has become part of British identity, but is served in ways that bear little resemblance to food in India or Pakistan.

Similar processes can occur in workplaces. It is common that new staff are hired because of the skills and knowledge that they have learned elsewhere, with a view to their teaching these to existing staff. Only rarely does this completely fail, or result in a complete change of practice. Most often some form of synthesis occurs. In scientific laboratories, it can often be surprisingly difficult to duplicate the experimental practices accomplished elsewhere, even when staff have been brought in for that purpose and training is instigated. Often it turns out that the problems are due to minor, unrecognised differences in procedure, which can be as simple as 'doing the washing up' differently.

In Chapter 10 we will look at teams. One of the main findings is that a workplace team is better made up of a range of different people suited to different roles, than of a highly cohesive group of people who are extremely similar. The roles you play at work can create your identity. Positive feedback loops occur as well as negative ones. For example, the person who knows a little more than others about computers is likely to become an informal source of advice to workmates. In consequence, he or she will tend to become even better informed, through practice and exposure to a range of computer problems. This will feed back and make it even more likely that their advice is sought. They may even end up as the IT officer, even though they did not begin thinking that they were interested in computers. In terms of identity, doing is being.

People routinely adopt different identities in different social groups; hence the idea of a social role

This is also a central theme of this book. Perhaps because of the inappropriate dualist division between the 'real' mind and the social 'role', people often tend to over-estimate the extent to which behaviour and identity are caused by stable internal personal factors. They also under-estimate the extent to which behaviour and identity are caused by the social situation. Chapters to follow will partly redress this balance. It is a commonplace mystery that people can 'be so different' in different social roles, but this is only a mystery if we continue to believe that there is a clear distinction to be drawn between the self and the roles that we fill. One's self, one's identity, is a narrative construction built on the social roles and experiences one has had, not some fixed core that existed and continues to exist somewhat independently of everyday social life.

Summary

We suggest that people's identities are formed by their interactions with other people. How other people see you affects how they treat you, which in turn affects how you treat them, which affects how they will see you in the future. These processes are subtle, continuous and interactive, so identity is a fluid process, not a fixed and permanent thing that you are stuck with. Your identity will vary depending upon what group you are in and your contributions to a group help form your own and the group's identity. Our stable personal identities are constructed to make sense of our lives and social relationships. This view is not dualist, but intersubjective. Rather than people 'reading' others and 'presenting' themselves, identity is socially negotiated during interactions.

Exercise

Your myth at work

You are going to construct a simplified personal myth about work (after McAdams, 1993). If you find this worthwhile, then you may want to look at McAdams's book. It is probably helpful to write the exercise down as you do it.

1   First of all, describe your career so far. If it were a book, then what chapters would your career contain? It might for example contain a chapter at school, another training and another on the job.
2   Now describe the best moment in your career so far. Why was it the best? Also describe the worst moment. Why was it so bad? What is the most vivid memory you have of your career?
3   Now we'll look at some of the characters in your myth. First, which person has had the most influence on your career? This might be choosing a career, or how you work, or somebody who helped you, or even be somebody whom you reacted against. It could be a parent, or a teacher, or a colleague, or somebody else. Second, which person has been the most troublesome in your career? Third, which person would you most like to be like at work?
4   Look over what you have written and think about the kinds of chapters, events and people you have chosen. Does this tell you anything interesting about how you see yourself at work? Have you learned anything else?

Recommended reading

Bandura, A. (1977) *Social Learning Theory*, Englewood Cliffs, NJ: Prentice-Hall.

Castells, M. (1998) *The Information Age: Economy, Society and Culture*, volumes 1–3, Oxford: Blackwell.

Goffman, E. (1959) *The Presentation of Self in Everyday Life*, Harmondsworth: Pelican.

Jenkins, R. (1996) *Social Identity*, London: Routledge.

Lacan, J. (1979) *The Four Fundamental Concepts of Psychoanalysis*, Harmondsworth: Penguin.

McAdams, D.P. (1993) *Stories We Live By. Personal Myths and the Making of the Self*, New York: Morrow.

Tajfel, H. (1981) *Human Groups and Social Categories*, Cambridge: Cambridge University Press.

Turner, J. (1987) *Rediscovering the Social Group*, Oxford: Blackwell.

7 The formation of groups

In the previous two chapters we looked at the ways that people rely upon other people and the groups they belong to for the development and maintenance of their personal identities. This chapter goes on to look at why and how groups form. Specific group purposes are as diverse as human interests and pursuits, so it is impossible to provide a list of why people do, might, or should work as a group. Instead, we will look at the basic and perhaps essential reasons for working as a group. We will then go on to look at how groups form and how they function socially as they form. Following chapters will look in more depth at specific aspects of group functioning and behaviour.

Objectives

By the end of this chapter you should:

- Appreciate the importance of groups at work.
- Know some of the different stage models of group formation.
- Understand the main concepts of psychodynamic theories of group formation.
- Be aware of the nature of cohesion.
- Know about formal and informal norms.
- Understand the nature of open communication.

Why do groups form for work?

Negative views of groups

Groups and meetings at work certainly can be wasteful of time and effort, frustrating and accomplish little. That appealing cynic Dilbert (Adams, 1997) portrays an organisational environment where meetings are 'a form of performance art' that accomplish nothing and where more effort is devoted to seeming to do something by writing reports about it and meeting objectives, than to actually doing any productive work. Such attitudes are common. We can summarise a whole range of different negative attitudes to group working as follows:

Perhaps groups could work, but in practice they are a complete waste of time and accomplish nothing   Groups only waste time if they function poorly or if personally you have no interest in anybody else's knowledge and ideas about anything. This is simply an excuse to avoid making any effort to change.

Groups are basically organised skiving that some people like because they can get out of doing any real work   This belies the substantial need for people to socialise at work, discussed further in Chapter 11. Even if 'bonding' and 'networking' are essentially socialising, and have no immediate productive output, they are essential to effective working. A workplace that prevents socialising will probably experience high staff turnover, with a subsequent lack of a trained and effective workforce.

Groups waste huge amounts of time talking about feelings and people's opinions   Who says that talking about feelings and opinions is a waste of time? By the end of this book you should realise that, on the contrary: *Failing* to talk about feelings and opinions is a huge waste of time. Of course genuine 'talking about' is not the same as cursory 'mentioning without being listened to' and it is the latter that is particularly dysfunctional.

Groups are a waste of time because senior managers make the real decisions elsewhere   Even if this is true, senior managers need the information that junior staff can provide, or their decisions may be stupid. Adams (1997) provides alarming and hilarious examples.

Groups are a necessary evil, because certain tasks cannot be accomplished any other way   Groups constituted as a necessary evil are likely to be half-hearted and somewhat dysfunctional (see Chapter 12). Insufficient time and effort will be put into them.

The positive alternative

Groups are absolutely essential to modern work and without them any enterprise is liable to flounder.

There are two reasons for this. First, groups happen whether or not they are 'supposed' to happen and ineffective groups cause huge problems.

An autocratic director and his 'yes-men' is a group, but one that is likely to make poor decisions and create a dissatisfied work force. People who work together on the 'shop-floor' will function as a group, whether or not their organisation has allowed for this to happen.

Second, according to Castells (1996–98), modern society relies upon the exchange of information to generate productivity and wealth. The most productive global format for enterprise is now 'the network enterprise' that consists of a network of different businesses linked in various ways, rather than the small or large autonomous organisation. A major advantage of the network enterprise is its flexibility in responding to the world's increasingly rapid changes in technology and market conditions. If Castells's (1996) account is accurate, then any workplace that believes that group communications are unnecessary is either (a) deluding itself about its working practices[1] or (b) risking failure by maintaining outmoded organisational practices. Group working is essential at the managerial level and may be desirable for all staff. Inept group working prevents effective use of networks and will rapidly lose productive advantage. Many managers spend most of their working time in groups of one sort or another (Handy, 1985).

Interdependence

We will not discuss the general advantages of socialisation at this point, but one specific purpose of group formation is worth highlighting. According to Lewin (1948) 'interdependence' is essential to the formation and successful functioning of any group. Lewin refers to 'interdependence of fate', when group members believe that their individual fate is dependent on the fate of the group at large. Later work on interdependence (Rabbie and Horwitz, 1969; Horwitz and Rabbie, 1982) suggests that it is important, but not essential, for group formation. The employees of a small company may believe that if the company fails they will all lose their enjoyable jobs, and this can give them unity of purpose to ensure the company's survival. Lewin also refers to 'task interdependence', where each member requires contributions from others in order to succeed at all. For example, to make and sell a sofa, you need a frame and upholstery. Neither the carpenter nor the upholsterer can make or sell sofas without the other.

Many groups also involve interdependence in another sense, which we will call 'role interdependence'. Many human activities simultaneously occur *in* a group and also *are* the group. That is, the activity is defined by the interaction of a number of different social roles and without at least some of the roles being present, the activity does not exist (Wicker, 1984). For example, one person can go for a run, but 'a race' consists of at least two people behaving in a certain way. It is a mistake to look at the runners, but ask where the race is, as if it were something separate.

Of the different roles, some are essential and define the group: for example, a committee usually requires that someone chair it and that someone acts as secretary and takes minutes. Other roles are optional: for example, there can be a number of people present who act neither as chair or secretary. More formal committees may specify a quorum of how many people must be present at minimum. Without at least a secretary, a chair and a quorate number of attendees, there is no committee. Similarly, a dinner party requires at least one host and one guest. If there are only two hosts – because the guests cancel – then that is not a dinner party and the hosts may even try to find new guests. A class requires at least one teacher and one student. If the teacher is absent then a student could take over. Many work activities require groups in this way. For example 'selling' involves some sort of interaction between a buyer and a seller and 'managing' involves a least one manager and one subordinate. Naturally, most work groups are a lot more complicated than this. For example, an appointments committee in a university may require the presence of:

1   a senior manager
2   the head of department where the appointment will be located
3   a member of the department
4   a personnel officer
5   a lay person
6   the head of another department; and
7   an external assessor from another university.[2]

Stages in group formation

Forming, storming, norming and performing

Having reviewed many studies of small group development Tuckman (1965) proposed that groups generally go through four clear stages of development as outlined in the order below:

Forming   A time of anxiety and confusion, members are just getting acquainted and may be wary of each other. This is the initial stage of group formation when members are establishing some ground rules and ascertaining what is acceptable and unacceptable behaviour. They will also be finding out about the group's purpose. We will use 'purpose' to cover all purposes, including explicit tasks, goals, duties, aims, objectives and mission statements.

Storming A time of hostility between individuals and sub-groups and rebellion against the leader (if there is one), or competition for the leadership role. Conflict about the group's rules and purpose may also occur. Opposing factions may form within the group.

Norming The time where norms and consensus about the purpose develop, cohesiveness emerges and a solid foundation is set for the group to achieve its purpose. Group members feel more relaxed about expressing their feelings and points of view within the group and group decisions are made. Members feel a sense of belonging to the group and develop more affinity with the other group members.

Performing The time when the group co-operates and focuses on successful performance of its purpose. The energy of the group is directed towards common and agreed goals. This will usually involve one or more kind of interdependence. An established group may perform well to serve its original purposes, but members may forget why they established their particular group norms, and also fail to recognise that the purposes they are serving are no longer valid. This can result in a group whose working practices are based on tradition and are not adequately reviewed.

Adjourning Tuckman added a fifth stage of development in 1977. Adjourning is the time when the group disbands and say farewells. If successful, the purpose will have been accomplished. Not all groups disband, some do not because their purpose is ongoing. Some groups try to stay together even when their purposes are over, because they have evolved to meet personal and social needs of members. This generally depends on the nature of the group and how long it has been together. Groups may continue to meet socially. Groups at work that have served their purpose may also try to stay together because:

- the group has become powerful;
- the work of the group is preferable to the work that members would return to;
- group members may fear redundancy; and
- the group has gained control of important resources, such as expenses budgets.

Norming is particularly important, as it is the stage when group members are willing to compromise and relinquish some of their own individual needs in favour of group coalition. Gelling may be viewed as a necessary process before the group can successfully carry out the tasks which have been set. Norming is also significant for the social dynamics of the group in that members may become more considerate and understanding of each other. Once the norming process is well under way any newcomer will undoubtedly experience some group pressure to conform to the established norms.

Tuckman's stages of group development make a lot of sense which most of us can relate to from our everyday group experiences. However, whilst his model is supported by the various small studies on group development that he surveyed, there are of course other perspectives on group development.

Other stage theories

Yalom's view (1985) is that groups go through three stages of development which are:

1   Orientation
2   Conflict
3   Cohesiveness.

These are not that different to Tuckman's forming, storming and norming stages, with no mention of performing, perhaps because Yalom did not look that far into group processes. Moreland and Levine (1994) looked at how a person enters a group, rather than group formation, and came up with stages that slice the transition similarly.

1   Evaluation – where the person considers whether the group is appropriate for them; similar to forming.
2   Commitment – where the person decides to become involved; replaces storming, as joining a pre-existing group limits the potential for conflict because the norms and purposes are already established.
3   Role transition – where the person begins to adapt to the group, takes on a role within the group and adapts their identity to fit the group; similar to norming.

Such stages provide useful and memorable descriptions of how groups form. As with other psychological stage theories, it is unlikely that the different stages will be distinct in practice; it is more realistic to see the stages as convenient ways of slicing and describing a continuous process. Although these stages are evidence-based, it is possible to question the extent to which groups develop in a stage-like fashion.

Psychodynamic accounts of group function

Horton (1999) provides a useful summary of psychodynamic theories of groups. Freud (1921) saw a group as following a leader – whom each group member had incorporated into their unconscious superego – and therefore identifying with each other in their egos. The superego is that part of the mind that provides social rules and norms. Freud is saying that a group unconsciously adopts a leader and uses him or her as a source of social rules and norms. Simplistically, this implies that each group chooses a member as leader, whether they know it or not. More realistically, a group might choose a set of norms and then embody them in a real, or even imaginary, person. For example, fan clubs may venerate a film or music star for what they represent to them, which may be far removed from what the star is really like as a person. Freud indeed distinguished between 'primitive' groups with an actual leader and 'secondary' groups who are 'led' by an abstraction. He also introduced a distinction between natural and artificial groups, where natural groups form and cohere entirely due to natural, internal forces, while artificial groups are held together by external forces. Almost all workplace groups are artificial; people generally have to work in those groups (or transfer) and cannot disband. Some research teams are examples of primitive groups in the workplace. The team is led by a clever and successful researcher, whose intelligence and energy motivate the team. However, there is a risk that the team will follow, right or wrong, and fail to develop themselves. Freud saw the followers as analogous to children. Secondary groups are probably more common at work and they may follow the 'mission statement' or other norms that they have established.

As with most aspects of Freudian theory, this view has some interest, but tends to blur the distinctions between literal ideas about group composition and purely symbolic ideas that could describe almost anything. If *any* group norms symbolise a leader, then all Freud is saying is that a group that has nothing in common is unlikely to stay as a group. The emphasis on leadership and shared, internalised norms also fails to recognise that many groups at work, and elsewhere, muddle along with many internal contradictions and difficulties. Workplace groups can function, perhaps, even when they contain colleagues who disagree violently and have not spoken for years. Groups can sometimes survive on task interdependence and role interdependence alone.

However, the general idea that groups come to internalise shared norms and perhaps act upon them unconsciously seems both plausible and important.

Bion (1961), disagreed with Freud's account, but emphasised that groups tend to operate on two levels. At the conscious level they work towards common purposes, but at the unconscious level they utilise 'myths' that serve to protect them when things go wrong. The *myth of dependency* is that the wise and strong leader exists to satisfy group members' needs. For example, the head of department should be able to sort things out. Helplessness and despair are produced when the 'leader' inevitably fails to live up to this ideal. Dependency allows group members to avoid taking responsibility themselves. Another common form of dependence is to rely upon the organisation's rule book whenever problems arise. The *fight-flight myth* is that an external enemy exists who must be attacked or avoided if the group is to survive. The group may promote an unofficial leader for the attack on another group member, or on something external. In many organisations it is tempting to blame 'the management' or 'the staff' when things go wrong. Again, this might be a way of evading responsibility. Finally, the *myth of pairing* is that the future will solve everything. The group regards two members as prophets who will lead them into the future and there is unrealistic hope expressed in vague and unsubstantiated generalisations. For example, workplaces sometimes expect that a new computer system will sort out all their administrative problems and that 'things will improve once we have installed and learned how to use the new package'. This avoids having to sort things out now and progress the group's purpose.

We doubt that these three basic assumptions are only and always present in groups. For instance, from our own experiences at work, we suggest that another unconscious myth can be *nostalgia*, where the group reminisces about the 'good old days' and spends a lot of time complaining about the present, but without acting. This tends to produce feelings of helplessness, sterility and futility. The group will work towards its purpose in a half-hearted manner if it progresses at all and may not take decisions seriously. As you saw in Chapters 4 and 5, people are creative in their personal (and probably group) myths and no simple scheme will easily capture all the myths groups may make.

Nonetheless, the general idea that the emotional needs of the group can interfere with the group's purpose is important. It also makes sense that this is more likely when things go wrong and that some of the misbehaviours that people can engage in during groups may be unconsciously motivated. According to Horton (1999) other theorists who have emphasised these points include Foulkes (1964) and Lewin (1948). We think that the key points are as follows:

- A group operates on both a conscious and an unconscious level, so the group's explicit purpose will not explain all its behaviour.
- When things are difficult, then the group can respond irrationally to protect itself, perhaps using the types of myth described by Bion (1961).
- The unconscious needs of some groups include a need for leadership of some kind.

Group cohesion and structure

The hierarchy

As a group is formed, different members will come to play different roles. Some will have essential roles and others inessential roles. Some members will have more responsible roles than others and usually as a result will have higher status/standing within the group. Factors such as knowledge, skill, ability, competence and experience will influence the exact position a member will acquire within a more formal group structure. However, other factors such as personality traits (e.g., outgoing, amicable) or social factors (good communicator, socially skilled) may also have an impact. Often members will demonstrate their status within the group structure with the aid of some of the non-verbal cues outlined in Chapter 3 such as dress, posture and other mannerisms. Other symbols are also used to highlight structure and hierarchy within groups. For example, the size of a group member's office and its arrangement can say a lot about the structure within a group; the more senior members may well have bigger, plusher offices than the less senior members who may have to share office space.

Generally the level of hierarchy within a group is a good predictor of how members communicate with each other. However, the more stable the group structure is, the better the communication network between members tends to be. Communication tends to occur more frequently between members who work closely together within the group structure. Generally more senior group members will communicate more with each other than with lower status members and are pivotal in the communication structure. They will tend to be privy to information that less senior members do not possess. It is quite uncommon that information is disseminated to all members simultaneously. Information can be regarded as a great source of power in groups: being aware of what is going on; being able to influence decisions made in the group. Indeed, access to information and higher status roles or (leadership roles) tend to go hand in hand in most group structures. Whilst this can be very rewarding for those members involved in this process, it can be equally frustrating for members who have little or no involvement in the communication structure at this level; all too often decisions are made with which they do not agree. However, this need not always be the case: in some group structures there is less focus placed on the hierarchical structure of the group and all members have a much more equal say in the communication process.

Perceived dominance

Following on from this, in many workplace groups, including meetings and committees, a key determinant of behaviour is the perceived dominance of group members. For example, if a senior manager is present then this may inhibit other people from speaking and make them tend to say only what the manager wants to hear. This may happen even if the manager would be happy to have a more frank and open discussion. People are reluctant to communicate openly in front of others who have power over them, because they fear the consequences. It is therefore important that the senior people in a meeting encourage open communication from others and ensure that people are rewarded rather than punished for open communication. Otherwise, despite their best intentions, open communication will not occur and groups will become speech-sessions for those perceived to be powerful, or sessions where everyone insincerely agrees with managers' opinions. It is one thing to say that open communication is encouraged, another to actually encourage it. Often, 'discussions' can degenerate into venues where the boss talks and the subordinates listen, or voice agreement.

As well as reflecting an existing dominance hierarchy, groups are also a key place where people try to assert their own dominance. Even when 'the boss' encourages open communication and wants other people's input into decisions, it is quite possible that some less dominant group members discourage others from being more open. Speaking out may be seen as 'sucking up' to the boss, or being disloyal to fellow workers. Or, subordinates may somewhat passively try to assert their own place in the dominance hierarchy by showing that they do not have to listen to their peers. It is not rare in meetings to see activities as overt as sighing, reading, looking out of the window, or whispering to neighbours when someone who is perceived as less important is speaking. The more dominant members of a group often have to actively encourage open communication by showing their verbal and non-verbal approval of communications made by all.

The opposite can also occur. People often seize a meeting as an opportunity to show off in an attempt to become more dominant within the group. This can be overdone and sometimes other people's signs of boredom are genuine. Some people in a group contribute more than they should, perhaps feeling that they have to say something about every topic raised, or feeling that they must never miss an opportunity to state their point of view, even when this is already well known to the rest of the group.[3] Chairing a group, whether formally, or informally as a more dominant group member, can involve discouraging some people from communicating too frequently. It is relatively easy to stop people from communicating at all, or stop them from attending the group, but more difficult to persuade people to communicate appropriately and relevantly. More skilled communicators will indeed be able to manage communication in groups to enhance their own dominance. This will involve saying appropriate and relevant things, as well as facilitating communications from other people. Failing to listen, going on too long, being too argumentative or becoming irrelevant will not endear you to other group members.

Group cohesion

This arises when a group becomes very close knit, as the group forms shared attitudes. Cohesive groups generally work more effectively together and members also work more effectively on individual tasks (Wech, *et al.*, 1998). There is some danger, however, that an extremely cohesive group will become a conformist group, and there are also dangers that the group will act irrationally to protect itself. Forgas (1985: 296) defines cohesion as the extent to which a group (1) shares norms and purpose, and (2) has members with positive sentiments about each other and their group. Some groups are cohesive mainly for the first reason – such as many workplace groups – others for the second – such as many families, where members may not always see eye-to-eye but love each other anyway.

Other factors also influence cohesion, including:

- That the group members share similar values and attitudes – it is easier to cohere with like-minded people.
- Shared history – one reason for adventure weekends as 'team-building' exercises.

- Mutual experiences of adversity – another reason for adventure weekends.
- Public personal commitment to the group – hence rituals such as the taking of vows of loyalty.
- How much effort it takes to join the group – groups that are seen as prestigious or difficult to get into tend to instil more loyalty in members.
- Effective communication within the group – see much of this book.

Although group cohesion often develops naturally, it can be difficult to engineer when a group has problems. Cohesive groups tend to be intolerant of deviant behaviours and tend to pressurise members towards conformity. This is because cohesiveness and conformity are two perspectives on the same process: to cohere one conforms.

It is also worth pointing out that not all groups at work need to be that cohesive. Some groups function primarily in terms of task interdependence – each person knows their duties and performs them efficiently and in harmony with the rest of the group. Fordist production line work is an obvious example. Although a production line or assembly crew can become a cohesive group, it can also operate successfully without much cohesion, particularly if they have opportunity for normal social interaction. Perhaps this situation is more likely when the group's purpose is externally-imposed. The production line workers do not decide what to make. When work groups need to determine their own purpose, then lack of cohesion will make it difficult for the group to adapt to change.

The establishment of group norms

Over time groups develop norms, which are unspoken rules regarding behaviour; what is and what is not acceptable. As already mentioned earlier in the book, to fit into the group it is generally a requirement to conform to its norms. Often people are not even consciously aware of group norms. However, whilst conforming to norms leads to friendship, respect and support, breaking norms can lead to being left out, becoming a target for jokes, nasty remarks and perhaps even more extreme measures such as being ostracised.

There are two types of group norm: formal and informal.

Formal norms

These norms of behaviour are often imposed externally and usually written. For example, a nation's laws, or formal rules and regulations for a school or university. The group may also write their own norms, as when a workplace lists key procedures on the wall. People often imagine that the formal norms of their group are based on reasoned principles and represent the best way of behaving. It can be revealing to travel elsewhere – even if only to another organisation – and discover that their rules are entirely different: one company may insist that all correspondence is funnelled through a team of secretaries, in order to give it a consistent style. Another company will insist that everybody handles their own correspondence.

Formal norms usually develop after group decision-making of some kind, although not necessarily by the group that the norms are imposed upon. However long they have been used and however wise they seem, formal norms are subject to the biases and problems of group decision-making that will be discussed in Chapter 8. Suffice to say that procedures, rules and laws were written by fallible people and should not be followed unquestioningly if they appear to be stupid, inappropriate or dated (see also Chapter 10).[4]

Informal norms

These norms of behaviour tend to be developed within the group and are frequently implicit. The best known example of this is from the 'Bank Wiring Group' in the 'Hawthorne studies' (Roethlisberger and Dickson, 1939), where workers set norms among themselves controlling output rate. However, these norms were well understood and strongly sanctioned.

A better, almost as well-known, example of implicit norms comes from Garfinkel (1967). Students were instructed to act at home as if they were a lodger – to speak formally and politely to the family. This led to strong negative reactions from families, including bewilderment, shock and embarrassment. Families told the students that they were being inconsiderate, selfish and mean (American 'mean' is 'unkind' in UK). We cannot help being amused by this, as many parents exert great effort to make their children polite. Clearly, the informal (and implicit) norms of interaction in most families are for a less-than-polite style of interaction (see Chapter 2) and deviations from this style were regarded as inappropriate and as failing to participate properly in family life.

Most workplaces have many such implicit norms, including how people dress (even when there is not an explicit dress code), how they communicate and their orientation to their work. The recent enquiry into police mishandling of their investigation of the murder of the black teenager Stephen Lawrence has popularised the notion of implicit, or institutional, racism, in the police and other organisations. The norms of a group can be implicitly racist (or sexist or otherwise inappropriate) without this ever being overtly discussed or agreed and without any of the individual people being consciously racist. A number of types of implicit group norm can perpetuate problems. We will continue to use implicit racism in the police as an example (see Holdaway, 1997):

Ignorance of outgroups   This can lead to misunderstandings and mis-interpretations that the group fail to recognise, or indeed use to confirm their norms. For example, Afro-Caribbean young men tend to spend a high proportion of their income on their cars. Young black men in expensive cars are perceived by the police to be drug dealers. A few are and the detection of these confirms the stereotype. The ignorance is not corrected because the group tend to share it and cohesion makes individuals reluctant to criticise.

Unquestioned background assumptions   The most basic values of a group are often so shared and ingrained that the group cannot recognise them. For example, the police may treat black people differently from white people, often switching between being excessively polite and friendly and being excessively hostile. They may feel hurt or offended when their attempts to be polite and friendly do not pay off and consequently become hostile. It does not help that few police are black, and that recuitment of black officers is not an easy task.

Humour and story-telling define the in-group and out-groups   Groups use stories to construct their worlds. Jokes and stories are used to confirm the group's implicit world-view and to warn about and define the boundaries of acceptable behaviour. In the police (and indeed elsewhere) racist 'jokes' confirm racism, while stories about badly-behaved black people establish norms. More subtly, stories about well-behaved black people also confirm the norm that they are usually badly behaved – the exception that 'proves' the rule. Stories often describe the opposite of whatever the group sees as mundane and routine.

Selective exposure   The group's experiences can be formed by prejudice and the experiences are then used to confirm implicit norms.

If the police arrest more black people, because they attend more to their activities, then they will see more black people passing through the criminal justice system, confirming that they are right to attend to them selectively.

The implicit nature of such processes can make it extremely difficult to effect major changes in prejudiced or otherwise inappropriate group norms. The group's norms constitute a coherent world-view that will tend to assimilate new information. Specific attitudes may be successfully challenged, but changes in specific attitudes may have little or no effect on the underlying group world-view. To tackle this, it may be necessary (1) to make the world-view explicit, (2) to get the group to admit this view and (3) to get them to agree to change it. Each of these steps will be hindered by group defence mechanisms, as well as by the fact that individuals need not have internalised the norms for them to function at the group level. Individuals will usually find it easy to deny that they believe such things, leaving the group norms intact, but nobody's responsibility. When groups are cohesive and have strong, inappropriate norms, then it may be easier to change working practices around them, ensuring that new staff are protected from the group norms and dispersing or moving the group so that it can do as little harm as possible. This appears so far to have proved impossible for the police to manage.

Part of group formation should be to encourage the group to be reflective and self-aware about the norms that they are developing. Most groups can develop norms and practices – even with the best intentions – that eventually work against the purposes of the group. If these norms have developed explicitly, then group members will feel some responsibility for them and they may be easier to change. Furthermore, if the group is free to discuss openly any and all concerns, then if undesirable implicit norms appear to be developing they can be raised and discussed. But groups can, unfortunately sometimes, set implicit rules on what they may discuss – and they may be quite blind to their own implicit norms.

Open communication

Open communication is more than everyone feeling free to speak. In a pub or party setting, communication is usually quite free, in the sense that everyone can easily speak, but it may not be open because people may be too busy speaking to communicate effectively with each other. Open communication in a group occurs when (1) everyone feels free to speak honestly, whatever the other group members have already said, or are known to believe, (2) everyone is listened to by the other group members, and (3) the group is able to reach consensus on most of its communicative tasks, despite disagreements.

Group communication is not open when

1   Some of the group say nothing, or only what they believe the others want to hear.
2   Some of the group are not listened to by other members.
3   The group either reaches a phoney consensus because no one will voice disagreement, or breaks down in the face of its disagreements.
4   Certain important topics are prohibited – such as questioning group attitudes, structure and purpose.

It is quite rare for a group to be open, for all members, all the time. From the material earlier in this chapter, you should appreciate that in most groups there will be tensions. While open communication facilitates group formation, both cohesiveness and the existence of a leader, or norms, will tend to discourage open communication when issues that threaten the group are involved. We will look further at open communication in Chapter 10.

Some groups appear cohesive on the surface, but only because dissent and discussion are prohibited. Communication will be closed rather than open. The group members may stay together only reluctantly because they feel interdependent. A group like this may function adequately for routine tasks, but will have difficulties adapting to change and new working practices. Indeed, the group's main purpose may be to preserve the status quo. Some democratic groups develop like this, particularly if members fear that open communication would be so divisive as to virtually destroy the group. It is however more common for such pseudo-cohesive groups to develop under the control of an autocratic manager.

Inhibition of communication in groups

Most people find that their communication skills are inhibited in groups at one time or another. Even people who are extremely experienced and skilled in one type of group may hesitate in another. There are many common causes.

Many people are generally anxious about communicating in front of several people and fear that they will be inarticulate, or judged negatively by some of those present. Almost everyone has felt anxious in front of a group at some time or other. The key way of tackling this anxiety is to practise contributing to groups. With experience, anxiety will generally fade, whereas if your anxiety makes you avoid saying anything then you will never gain the experience to reduce anxiety. You may have to practise your contribution to a group in advance the first few times that you want to say something. Being practised will make you more confident and clearer when you speak, which will make it a more positive experience.

In any group, new members are somewhat uncertain about the group's informal and formal rules of conduct. How is one supposed to speak, formally or informally, briefly or at length? How should people be addressed, first name, surname, or even by role? 'Madam Speaker' in the House of Commons will be displeased to be called 'Betty'. What topics of conversation are allowed? Can one make jokes, or should one be entirely serious? Who plays which role within the group? Some people may require more careful handling than others. Most new members will be quieter at first in a group than they will be after a few meetings.

Sometimes, the group itself is new and everyone is uncertain about the rules. Most professionally run groups use ice-breaker material to try and get people communicating and may try to set explicit rules for the group to operate by. Ice-breakers also try to get groups to know each other (see exercises).

Another inhibitor in a group can be uncertainty about one's personal role in the group. For example, you may understand clearly that you are there as the representative of your department, but be unclear whether everything you say should support your department, or whether you can express your personal opinions. Role uncertainty can be quite substantial in some groups, because it is never all that clear who all the other group members are and what their roles are supposed to be. Are they all representing departments, like yourself, or are they there for different reasons? For example, you were simply told to go to the SCID (Section Co-ordinating and Information Dissemination) meeting on Monday. You had ten minutes to prepare and know virtually nothing about it. Generally speaking, groups where the members know each other personally to some extent will communicate more openly. On the other hand, a group where some members know each other well can make other members' roles even less clear. The more friendly members may slip in and out of formal and informal communications in a way that is inappropriate amongst people who are less familiar with each other.

It also takes time to learn appropriate behaviour within a group. Groups tend to have both explicit and implicit norms about appropriate behaviour and these are not always easy to work out from observing other people's behaviour. For example, if the chair is doing most of the talking is this because other group members are not supposed to speak, or because no one else has anything to contribute at that point? It is often sensible for new group members to ask whether it is appropriate for them to speak at that moment, or on that topic. Norms about interruptions also vary. Some groups may tolerate, even expect, a high rate of interruptions and interpret failure to interrupt as lack of interest or shyness. Other groups may expect everyone to be allowed to have their say in peace and regard interruption as rude or arrogant. Again, when in doubt it may be best for new members to ask! One warning though; in many groups the implicit norms are not the same as the explicit norms. The managing director may tell everyone that they are free to interrupt whenever they like, but make it extremely clear that interruptions are unwelcome when they actually occur.

It may also be difficult to judge the extent to which emotionality is regarded as appropriate in a group. Workplace groups often seem anti-emotional and members are supposed to display calmness and confidence, suppressing strong feelings, or only expressing strong positive feelings. Another common inhibitor of communication is the fear of expressing inappropriate emotions. Someone who feels very angry about what another person has said may keep silent out of fear of being clearly angry. In groups where communication is effective, there tend to be mechanisms for expressing 'inappropriate' emotions. These are discussed in Chapter 11. Generally speaking it is more effective to say how something makes you feel than to either avoid communicating, or to simply express the emotion. It can be more helpful to say 'That makes me feel angry because ...' explaining why, than to explode with rage. However, many people have difficulty acknowledging and expressing their emotions in such ways.

A further inhibitor of communication can be a fear of showing one's ignorance. Many groups have developed special jargon and expertise, which can seem intimidating to a newcomer. Again, when in doubt the assertive response is to ask – you will find that jargon is often confusing to everybody.

Deterring open communication

Often, managers shut down communication without realising it. Some common techniques are:

- Ask 'Any questions?', but do not wait long enough for questions to emerge.
- Ask 'Any questions?', or say that open communication is welcome, but criticise or attack any statements made by others with which one disagrees. This punishes open communication and it will rapidly cease.
- Say that other people's concerns are irrelevant, or display impatience with them. Or, specify a very narrow range for discussion that presupposes most of the basic issues.
- Show disapproval by non-verbal cues, such as sighing, looking bored or attending to other tasks.

Open communication is hollow if it does not include the expression of dissident, doubting and critical views.

Facilitating open communication

- Allow and schedule adequate time for questions in meetings.
- Tolerate other people's views and make sure that you praise their efforts, even if you disagree with them.
- Let the entire group be the 'jurors' on what is relevant and irrelevant, rather than being an authoritarian 'judge' of relevance.
- Suppress non-verbal signs of disapproval.
- Use the communication techniques covered in Chapters 2 and 3 to question, listen and reflect effectively.

These techniques do not just apply to managers!

Conclusions

In this chapter we have looked at how and why groups form and some of the benefits and problems that can occur. Groups often become cohesive, so that group members become more similar to each other, members consider their membership to be an important part of their personal identities and the group develops a positive sense of itself. While cohesive groups tend to perform better in the workplace, they can also function poorly, particularly when the group is felt to be under threat and we will look further at group functioning in the next few chapters. The development of cohesion is facilitated by open communication between group members.

Exercises

Bion's myths

Think about your experiences in groups at work. Can you think of examples where groups behaved irrationally in the ways theorised by Bion? Remember these are 'dependency', 'fear-flight' and 'pairing'. We added 'nostalgia'. What happened as a result of these mythical processes?

Reading the hierarchy

Think about the group structure of a formal and an informal group you are a member of, or have been a member of in the past. Consider how the roles of different group members are manifested through signals such as dress code, seating arrangements, other non-verbal behaviour and communication structure, for example, access to information.

Implicit norms

This exercise is best done with other people from a real work group. Working by yourselves, write down three implicit values that you feel are shared by your work group. These could be general attitudes to work like 'have a laugh' or 'don't let them get you down'. Or they might be attitudes to out-groups, such as customers, clients or senior managers. Or they might be implicit rules about how your work should be done, such as 'customer first, paperwork last' (or vice versa).

Ice-breaking

There are many tasks which group leaders can use to get people communicating with each other. A simple ice-breaker involves each member of the group introducing themselves to the group and perhaps stating how they see their role and objectives in the group. A more sophisticated task would be to divide the group into pairs. The pairs get to know each other for a few minutes, then each member has to introduce the other one to the group. This encourages more complex communication than mere introductions, which can involve as little as a single sentence.

Recommended reading

Bion, W.R. (1961) *Experiences in Groups and Other Papers*, London: Tavistock.

Handy, C.B. (1985) *Understanding Organizations*, New York: Facts on File.

Horton, M. (1999) 'Working with groups', in D. Messer and F. Jones (eds) *Psychology and Social Care*, London: Jessica Kingsley.

Horwitz, M. and Rabbie, J.M. (1982) 'Individuality and membership in the intergroup system', in H. Tajfel (ed.) *Social Identity and Intergroup Relations*, Cambridge: Cambridge University Press.

Moreland, R.L. and Levine, J.M. (1994) *Understanding Small Groups*, Boston, MA: Allyn and Bacon.

8 Social influence in groups

How people behave in a group depends on both the other people present and on some basic rules of social influence. Group behaviour is not just the behaviour of each person, added together. This chapter will look at the basic processes of social influence and indicate how these affect behaviour in groups.

Objectives

By the end of the chapter you should:

- Know the main forms of social power.
- Appreciate the relative nature of authority and the difficulties of defining leadership.
- Understand the main mechanisms of normalisation, conformity, obedience and de-individuation.

Sources of individual power in groups

Power is one important aspect of social influence. Indeed, when someone can influence others then we often say that he or she has power over them. Power comes from both really having sources of power and from display of power. Often, display of power is more than enough in itself.

Physical power

Power can come from simple physical force – do what I say, or I'll hit you, or get my soldiers to hit you – or from the threat of such force, but physical power can also come without any such threat. Taller people tend to be more successful in life, along with a minority of very short people who are believed to overcompensate. Many people would be annoyed to be judged on their size rather than their abilities, but does tallness suggest physical power and make others more likely to listen to a tall person? Studies in which people rate others find that taller people tend to be rated as more intelligent and capable.

In the workplace – other than in sports and the armed forces – real physical power is rarely relevant and people who are openly physically intimidating are unlikely to succeed, but suggesting physical power may influence others, even if the display has no real basis. There has been advice to the business community on power dressing – wear dark colours, look tall, fit and serious – and power lunching (eat food that suggests predation and health, such as meat and raw food). One has to be careful not to overdo such displays and be seen as a crank or show-off, rather than as powerful. Senior managers may wear expensive dark suits, but if the junior clerk copies them then he may be teased. Still, when entering a new group it is useful to give some thought to your physical presentation of self (see Chapter 3).

Economic power

Economic power is also important, including the ability to hire or fire people. As with physical force, the threat of economic power – such as feeling that someone in the group can influence promotion prospects – can be more important than the actual power wielded. It is also quite common in workplaces for people to wield power over others in the form of economic benefits. The departmental secretary may control access to the stationery cupboard and use this to wield limited power over more senior staff. If a group contains people who have a track record of wielding economic power over others present, then it will be difficult to prevent them from controlling the group, whether that is what they want or not.

Sometimes, a group contains people who could, in theory, have such power, but do not exercise it: the department manager has never fired anyone and cannot do so without very good reason. Others may nonetheless behave as if this power were important. Some managers may encourage this, others may prefer not to be seen as powerful in that way. It can be helpful to distinguish between hints or displays of economic power and the real thing.

One common difficulty is that some staff base their behaviour on assumptions about what management will do if staff are open and truthful with them. Usually, they assume that management will punish disagreement, admission of mistakes, expression of doubts or the pointing out of problems with new projects. Sometimes such fears are justified, but often staff beliefs have never been tested. Good management should welcome and encourage openness. Unfortunately, managers sometimes say that they encourage openness, but appear to fail to reward it, or even punish it. Group dynamics can be subtle and it is not always easy to tell what the consequences of speaking out are. It can be damaging to an organisation if the perception amongst staff is that openness is punished, or toadying to management is rewarded. Such perceptions can occur falsely, but when they occur it is wise for management to ask themselves if, despite their best efforts, they have been susceptible to flattery or hurt by criticism.

Control of information

People can wield power because of the knowledge that they possess and because of their ability to manage how information is disseminated. The heads of global media organisations, such as Rupert Murdoch, can exert power over governments because of the damage that their organisations can do by providing adverse or critical publicity, or withdrawing positive publicity. At a more pedestrian level, managers' secretaries often wield considerable power in an organisation by their ability to control access to the manager and to disseminate important information (officially, or unofficially).

In work it is difficult to pretend that one wields physical or economic power, if one does not. It is therefore a common ploy for people to pretend to have more control over knowledge and information than they really do, in order to suggest that they are powerful. Common devices include:

- 'Name-dropping' and otherwise suggesting that you have the ear of the really powerful.
- Gossiping and passing on gossip to show that you really know what's going on.[1]
- Keeping knowledge of vital procedures to yourself, or developing methods of operating that only you can understand – don't file things alphabetically for example.
- Using impenetrable specialist jargon to sound well-informed. Medicine and computing are common offenders here.
- Refusing to explain your specialist area in terms anybody else can understand.

While these devices are unhelpful if taken to extreme, if you never use any of them, you risk being undervalued, as your colleagues consider that you don't have influence, or know what's going on, and that your work could be done by anybody. It is useful to show off knowledge a little.

Authority and leadership

In a group, a person's authority is defined by their status in terms of all the sources of power mentioned earlier, but also in terms of their role in the group. In a committee the chair has authority, even if the person occupying the chair has little other power. At work people often use (or abuse) roles of authority, such as the chair, the group secretary, the safety officer, or the purchasing officer, to promote and advance their personal power. Authority is often signalled quite clearly in more formal groups. Some committee rooms have larger chairs, reserved for the chairperson. Regal audience rooms contain thrones. Presidents of some learned societies wear special chains or medals of office. Some social roles of authority have special uniforms. Doctors often wear white coats, different classes of nurse have different uniforms, the police have special uniforms and so on.

Most of us realise that out of uniform, under the white coat or without the chains of office, the policewoman, doctor or mayor are quite ordinary people. However, when they are in role there is pressure for people to respect authority. Later on we will look at obedience to authority.

The ways that people use the trappings of authority are interesting. People whose power comes mostly from the authority of their role often make the most of this and use whatever signs are available. People who have considerable power from other sources often choose to reject the visible signs of authority. Detectives do not wear police uniforms. Is this because they really have to be undercover, or because they are showing that their power is based on more than a uniform? Powerful heads of state and business sometimes choose to break the dress codes of those who are merely in authority, perhaps to emphasise that, unlike their managers, they are truly powerful, not merely by virtue of their social role. The media tycoon Robert Maxwell would often wear a tracksuit but his executives still wore business suits.

The qualities of leadership perhaps involve the aspects of authority that are non-symbolic and positive. It is commonly imagined that being a leader involves exceptional personal characteristics, but as mentioned in Chapter 5, research has failed to confirm this. It is possible that leadership is more of an attribute of a social role than of the person filling that role. While there has been a lot of research on strong, good or charismatic leaders, there has been less on people whose leadership has clearly failed. One wonders if they might not display exactly the same qualities and deficiencies as 'good' leaders, except that the projects they led did not work out. However, as we will see later on in this chapter, it is apparently commonplace and probably socially functional for people in a group to obey a leader. As we saw in Chapter 7, it may also serve the emotional needs of the group to follow a leader. We are not suggesting that absolutely anybody can lead, merely that the role forms the person more than the person strengthens the role. We will look further at different kinds of role that might involve some of the qualities of 'leadership' in Chapter 11.

The influence of the majority

Much research in social psychology has shown that when individuals get together in collective settings they easily conform with the majority and abandon or suspend their own attitudes and values. Research has focused on attempting to understand why we are so willing to conform to rules imposed on us by the groups to which we belong, whether a small group of friends or a factory floor. Various studies have investigated what processes underlie our need to conform to the norms of group behaviour.

According to Forgas

> The most astounding fact about conformity is that groups of people will tend to develop shared, consensual ways of behaving and seeing the world almost automatically, even when there are absolutely no objective reasons for doing so.
>
> (Forgas, 1985: 273)

Normalisation

Sherif (1935) illustrated the tendency to develop group norms using the 'autokinetic phenomenon', which is that a single, small fixed light source in a totally dark room will appear to drift about as your eyes move, because you can see nothing else to relate it to. As there is no fixed visual reference, people asked to estimate how much the light is moving give widely different estimates ranging from centimetres to over a metre. However when a group of people do the task together and communicate, then they quickly converge on a single value – which also varies widely across groups – despite the fact that they are communicating on an artificial and arbitrary task in the pitch darkness. Groups of people rapidly tend to agree, rather than begging to differ. In the workplace, normalisation is usually implicit and involves a shared view of the world of which the group may not be fully aware. This does not mean that groups do not argue about things, but even arguments tend to assume group norms.

For example, teaching staff in schools can be collectively quite negative about parents in regard to the education of their children: Parents are seen as either uninterested and neglectful, or over-concerned and interfering. Teachers will disagree about 'what kind of parents' a particular child has, but will rarely dispute the general assumptions made about parents. As we will see, it is common for groups to define their norms in part by despising others outside the group. In private, the recipients of a group's services are often depicted as stupid, unco-operative, ignorant and worthless, whether they are students, customers, patients, computer users, clients or the people whose offices you clean. It can be problematic when such depictions are taken too seriously.

In most workplaces, norms are also developed about working practices that govern such issues as how tasks should be undertaken and how fast work should occur; we have already mentioned the 'Bank Wiring Group's' norms about output rate in Chapter 7. Such norms do not only apply in monotonous, relatively unskilled work. For example, academic staff in universities are expected both to teach and to conduct research that leads to publications. The norm is to produce a balance of both activities. Staff who teach but fail to publish are explicitly sanctioned in most departments. Staff who research but teach poorly, or get out of teaching, are resented – as they make work for others – and may be informally sanctioned. Staff who publish 'too much' may also be resented, as they make their less prolific colleagues look bad. At minimum, they will be criticised behind their backs for their lack of a home or social life. The same applies to staff who appear to go to too much trouble to prepare teaching; this can raise standards for the students, but possibly worsen working conditions for staff.

Conformity

Beyond the establishing of group norms, do people also conform to group beliefs? In a famous series of studies Asch (1955) got people to make a judgement about the length of different lines in a group setting where the rest of the group were stooges told to make a judgement

that contradicted what could be seen. Stooges first made correct judgements that the subject had no difficulty agreeing with. Only a quarter
of subjects never went along with the incorrect group judgement.
Afterwards, most subjects revealed that they knew that the judgement
was wrong, but went along with it anyway – they had judged correctly
but they had agreed to fit in. Some subjects – reasonably under the
circumstances since we don't often encounter groups of people lying to
us about what we can see – doubted their own perceptions.

It is also interesting that this susceptibility to group pressure got
stronger as group size increased from one other person, to two or three
other people, but did not increase after that. Apparently it is easier
to contradict one person than two or more. Another phenomenon
was that if one of the stooges was instructed to go against the group
and report the correct judgement, then this greatly reduced conformity. Attempts to replicate this work in the 1970s got mixed results
that suggested that to some extent conformity is culturally determined.
Students in the 1950s were more respectful and conforming than in
the 1970s, when conformity was found to be weaker and more dependent on the exact social situation.

The basic phenomenon still exists however. It may be due to a
number of mechanisms. First, the tendency to use other people as
sources of information – to imitate them because they may know more
than we do. Situations like the Asch studies are extremely unusual.
Normally other people are reliable sources of information. If they
disagree with us, then it is rational to wonder if we are mistaken. If
you enter a new situation and everybody seems to be behaving
strangely then perhaps you should imitate them until you can work
out what is going on.

Second, the strong desire to fit in and get along with people. Studies
of kidnapping and torture find that in these extreme situations the
victims often come to identify with their kidnappers or torturers, in
part because they are the only company they have and because they
have extreme shared experiences. Most people would rather get along
with anyone, than get along with no one. Such pressures are probably
stronger in a workplace than in a brief, artificial experiment with
people you will never see again.

Third, that conformity is often explicitly rewarded, while deviance
or dissent is punished. The most common mechanism for reward or
punishment is social approval or disapproval.

In everyday life, conformity must be more complicated than in
Asch's experiments because there is rarely the same certainty about
the judgement. We are not often expected to deny what we see and

are rarely faced with a group of people who are insincerely disagreeing with us. Most of the time pressure to conform comes when all the people in the group are somewhat uncertain about what to decide or believe and everyone decides to go along with a perceived norm. Sometimes this involves conforming to beliefs that nobody privately holds. For example, the sacrament in Christian mass requires the belief that wine has become, or can symbolise, the blood of Christ. The ceremony can take place (and perhaps often does) even if everyone involved, including the minister, privately doubts this belief. If this was discussed and debated prior to each mass, then mass would occur less often. As it is each person involved assumes that most other people have the relevant belief.

At work, many innovations and new developments occur despite each individual involved having serious private doubts about the course of action. Indeed perhaps innovation often requires the suspension of private disbelief. In Chapter 11 on teams, we will see that effective teams need to agree shared goals and perhaps any group requires some shared goals, beliefs or ideas before it will function as a group at all.

Yet, when everyone conforms to the status quo, because they assume that everyone else approves of it, then this can hold back development and may lead to the uncritical perpetuation of poor practices. Sometimes group working practices have evolved without any clear rationale and are then maintained for conformity alone.

Obedience to authority

Stanley Milgram, in a famous series of studies, demonstrated that people are willing to obey the orders of authority figures, even when this involves hurting other people in a manner with which they disagree. In his experiments, people were asked to give other people electric shocks to 'train' them on learning tasks. In the role of 'teacher' people were willing to give shocks, purely because the experimenter told them to and continued even when the stooge being 'shocked' (no shocks actually being administered) pretended to cry out in pain, demanded to be released and eventually went quiet. People would often express concern, but would continue to increase the strength of the supposed shocks nonetheless when the experimenter 'reassured' them with the following set phrases. If the 'teacher' was still reluctant after the first phrase, then the experimenter said the second and so on.

'Please continue.'
'The experiment requires that you continue.'

'It's absolutely necessary that you continue.'
'You have no other choice, you must go on.'

Milgram had actually expected most people to refuse to continue after these rather feeble reassurances, but very few refused. This basic effect occurred across a wide spectrum of different people and even – to a lesser extent – when Milgram set up the experiment in a dodgy-looking warehouse, rather than in a university department. The experimenter also reassured the teachers that he would take full responsibility for their actions. Obedience also occurred despite the fact that most subjects believed that they really were shocking their students.

Factors influencing obedience

The profile of results across a total of nineteen experiments revealed that there were specific factors which influenced obedience:

- Proximity to victim: obedience decreased the nearer the victim was to the teacher.
- Proximity to experimenter: obedience increased if the experimenter was nearer the teacher and more surveillant.
- Environmental influences: obedience increased the more important or prestigious the surroundings were.
- Group pressure: obedience either increased or decreased depending on what a group of stooge subjects did.

Hurting others in obedience to authority appears to involve de-individuation in two ways. First, it is easier when the other people are not seen to be 'real' people. Second, it is easier when a person feels that they are being the agent for another person or organisation who is ultimately responsible for what happens. Thus, both the perpetrator and the victim are seen as less than fully human.

De-individuation has been confirmed in studies of how people are trained to be torturers. Torture is often conducted by a socially isolated group of people. They associate mostly with each other, are often crude and ill-educated in their view of the world and form a cohesive social group (although they are usually cruel towards each other as well) that sees others as less than human. It helps if they are rewarded for torturing, or its outcome.

Whilst Milgram's experiments may seem ethically wrong such obedience to authority has been dramatically demonstrated time and time again in society at large. Most social psychology books mention Nazi

Germany at this point; indeed understanding that phenomenon was one of Milgram's motives for his experiments. However, obedience to authority occurs routinely in the workplace, although not, we hasten to add, in the form of torturing other people, whatever your coffee break fantasies!

One difference between experiments and the everyday world is that among the motives for obedience in the everyday world are realistic fears about the power wielded by authority figures. Some atrocities in concentration camps were performed by prisoners, who committed them to avoid being executed themselves. Some guards may well have been motivated in part by the fear of losing their jobs, or being sent to the Russian front. Milgram's experiments however illustrate that people will obey even when no such sanctions can be imposed on them.

Obedience at work

People often do things for their employer that they would probably not do in their own right, including telling massive lies, breaking health and safety regulations, selling goods to people who do not want them, assessing or judging others in unfair ways and overcharging people for goods or services. An extreme example is the tobacco industry. It is now clear that people in the tobacco industry have known for a long time that cigarettes caused lung cancer, but they nonetheless continued to promote the product and play down the harm that it caused.

What are the excuses that people use for harmful 'obedience to authority' at work? They seem to us to be very similar to the thinking of Milgram's subjects.

> *De-individuation – passing on responsibility:*
>
>> 'It's not down to me, it would be more than my job is worth if I did it differently.'
>>
>> 'I'm sorry but it's company policy.'
>>
>> 'We don't have the resources to do it differently.'
>>
>> 'According to the computer your order has already been delivered to you.'
>
> *De-individuation of the people harmed:*
>
>> 'They can afford it.'
>>
>> 'They are too stupid to notice.'

'They are too lazy to haggle or shop around, so it's only what they deserve.'

'They are only tourists.'

Setting group norms:

'All companies overcharge clients for this.'

'It is standard industry practice.'

'If we didn't cut corners then we'd never make any profit.'

'It is our job to describe it in the best possible light.'

Reaping rewards:

'Our branch had the highest sales figures for last year.'

'The company is doing very well.'

'Students are not the ones who promote me.'

Such pressures are often genuine. Should they be? There is some evidence that when a workplace places employees under pressures like this, then it is reflected in costly high levels of staff dissatisfaction and turnover. In so far as Milgram's experiments can be generalised, it is important to realise that many of us are all too willing to obey, even when no harm will actually befall us if we do not.

Obedience is not, of course, restricted to hurting others. Orne (1962) in studying the power of psychological experiments found that people were willing to do meaningless and pointless things simply because they were taking part in an experiment. For example, subjects were told to work through a pile of sheets of simple arithmetic problems and then turn over an instruction card that read 'Tear up paper and start again'. Some subjects remained on these boring tasks for over five hours. Hopefully you do not think that your workplace is modelled on this experiment. Still, many of us spend at least some time at work doing things that seem pointless, simply because management asks us to do so. For example, universities tend to be fond of requesting lots of different returns of basic information about staff research and teaching activities. Most of these never seem to be used for anything.

Roles and de-individuation

In the well-known 'Stanford Prison experiment' in 1973, Philip Zimbardo had students role-play prisoners and guards in a mock jail. Zimbardo was interested in how influential roles can be. He was specifically interested in two major roles in prison: inmates and guards. Volunteers were recruited from the student population and were told that it was a two week experiment on maintaining law and order and on keeping 16 prison rules. They were paid $15 a day. Volunteers were randomly assigned to the role of prisoner or guard. The prison itself was set up in the basement of the psychiatric department where Zimbardo worked.

Every effort was made to make the simulated prison as realistic as possible with prison procedures enforced. The prisoner volunteers were arrested, taken to prison and stripped of individual identity. Identical uniforms were worn, they were given a number and told to address each other by number not name. The guards and prisoners were both made as anonymous as possible. The guards were expected to police the prisoners and were given a thorough briefing on how to implement rules and discipline although any form of corporal punishment was forbidden. The arrest procedure and booking procedure were extremely realistic. The manipulations worked very well and soon the prisoners began to lose their identity:

> 'I began to feel I was losing my identity. I was number 4 and I was really my number.'

Guards became aggressive and similarly they began to fit into their role. They became more aggressive and abusive and the conditions rapidly became very bad. The prisoners became depressed and passive and were released after six days when Zimbardo, stunned by the disturbed behaviour he was observing, including an impending prison riot, felt he had no choice but to terminate the experiment. The study was abandoned because the roles were played *too well*. Whilst he expected the volunteers to adopt their assigned roles he was astounded by how swiftly this occurred.

The Stanford Prison experiment has often been used as an example of de-individuation. Indeed Zimbardo himself concluded that the volunteers had undergone a process of de-individuation. Anonymity had led to a loss of identity that resulted in intense and rapid behavioural changes. The anonymity also divested them of normal social responsibility resulting in more erratic and irrational behaviour. The experiment illustrates how easily people are willing to conform to group pressures and adopt the expected behaviour of the group; with one group taking on a much more powerful role than the other. The results of this study were so shocking that Zimbardo subsequently began to argue for prison reform.

De-individuation is not restricted to such extreme circumstances. A large number of studies in social psychology have found that in groups people tend to behave according to role expectations for the group and hence behave differently.

Conclusions

In this chapter we have seen that in groups there are a number of strong pressures to fit in, to conform and to adopt whatever role you are supposed to play. Fitting into a group at work, or elsewhere, may meet people's basic social needs, although this is an area that would benefit from research other than from the psychodynamic tradition (see Chapter 7). In most workplaces, *real* power is wielded and many people fit in and conform for fear that they will otherwise be punished, or fail to be rewarded. Almost everybody's self-image is that they are a unique individual, who is superior in a number of ways to the typical person and has a good sense of humour (as the personal adverts say). There is a substantial body of research that shows that people can be like this, but simultaneously prone to conform, even excessively, when operating in a group. The group pressures described in this chapter apply to everyone, including yourself and your mates, as well as your more sheep-like colleagues. In chapters to follow, we will look at how groups work and discover that uncontrolled conformity can lead to problems.

Exercises

Peer pressure and conformity

For this exercise you need to think of two occasions when you were under pressure at work to agree with other people. One occasion when your opinion was clearly in the minority and another opinion was clearly the majority view. A second occasion when your opinion was clearly in the minority, but there was no clear majority consensus.

What was the outcome in each case, and how did it differ?

What factors led you to change your opinion, or go along with another opinion?

Obedience to authority

Think of a time when you obeyed an authority at work, even when you knew that your obeying was wrong in some sense – for example, morally wrong, or to the disadvantage of the organisation. Did you assume that the authority had power over you, or was power explicitly wielded?

How did you justify your decision to yourself?

How did you justify it to other people?

To what extent can you recognise the mechanisms described in this chapter in your response?

De-individuation

Assess the extent to which you are de-individuated at work. What is your role and does it carry clear role expectations that you conform to, or that others expect you to conform to? Are you seen primarily as your role? Have you ever behaved in ways that are 'in role' but not typical of you?

Recommended reading

Aronson, E. (1992) *The Social Animal*, sixth edition, New York: Freeman.

Forgas, J. P. (1985) *Interpersonal Behaviour; The Psychology of Social Interaction*, Sydney: Pergamon Press, pp. 267–88.

Kelman, H.C. and Hamilton, V.L. (1989) *Crimes of Obedience: Towards a Social Psychology of Authority and Responsibility*, New Haven and London: Yale University Press.

9 Group decision-making

While it is important to know how and why groups form and operate, at work most groups function to make and implement decisions of various kinds. As we will see in this chapter, group decision-making has certain advantages, but can be flawed. Moreover, in order to make sound decisions it is important that the group functions well, as a group. It is generally not possible to set up a group at work to make decisions, without considering the other aspects of group functioning that we have looked at so far. Groups that do not get on, do not communicate openly, or are run autocratically are more likely to make poor decisions.

Objectives

By the end of this chapter you should:

- Appreciate the advantages of group decision-making.
- Know the main problems that can occur, including risky shift, polarisation and 'groupthink'.
- Understand the processes that underlie group decision-making.
- Know some of the traps to avoid in group decision-making.
- Know some techniques for making better decisions in groups.

Decision-making within groups

Many decisions are made in groups rather than by individuals on their own; often it is assumed that a more balanced decision can only be accomplished by a group of people. Some groups are specifically designed for decision-making, including committees, juries, government bodies and quangos, health care teams and company boards. Most groups at work will have to make some decisions and groups have been found to make 'better' decisions than individuals in some situations. Some of the perhaps obvious advantages to group decision-making compared with just one person are that a group can have:

- Complementary knowledge and expertise.
- A broader range of experience and skills.
- The ability to generate more ideas in brainstorming sessions.
- The ability to generate more information on a problem.
- The ability to divide and share work.
- The ability to detect each others' mistakes.
- The ability to evaluate and correct possible decisions.
- Increased commitment and motivation because of group coherence.

All these things can be true, and it is also true that many decisions have to be made in a group because that is the democratically agreed form of the decision-making process. In some groups, individuals bring suggested decisions to the group, for discussion and formal approval. Usually there is little discussion and approval is granted, but this nonetheless represents an important check on individual activity.

Given these positive aspects of group decision-making you would think that groups would generally make more balanced decisions than individuals, because the range of views present are likely to eliminate any extreme or unreasonable options. Yet, it has been suggested in Chapter 8 that individuals within groups are influenced by conformity and obedience and may go along with unreasonable commands. So how exactly do you think that will influence group decision-making? This chapter will explore some of the issues involved.

Individual decisions versus group decisions

As already mentioned, one might expect that more rational or sensible decisions would be made by a group of people, rather than leaving it in the hands of one individual. However, whilst various studies have shown that individual decisions and attitudes often differ from group decisions and attitudes, groups may not necessarily make 'better' decisions than individuals. There has also been work on individual problem-solving versus group problem-solving (see Steiner, 1972) which reveals different effects. Table 9.1 provides a list of some of the common reasons why group decision-making is not necessarily better than individual decision-making.

Table 9.1 Reasons for poor group decision-making

Group members are too similar and do not bring a range of skills, knowledge and experience to the problem.

Group members are too different from each other to allow a common framework for effective communication.

Too many members in the group (more than about seven) limits individual participation.

Failure in group discussion to detect the skills and experiences of different members.

Group discussions can be too time consuming.

Time may be lost because of the social issues in the group. Individuals working on their own can concentrate solely on the task, not the task plus social interactions.

Individual members may dominate the others and conformity pressures can be strong enough to eliminate constructive criticism.

Conjecture may lead the group into irrelevancies and waste time.

As attitudes are formed collectively in a group, group members' individual attitudes tend to become more extreme than they were to begin with. This is in part because the group's opinions are not the moderate average of all the members' opinions, but those opinions that the group feel represent them and which they can all agree upon to some extent. Even when these attitudes are arbitrary or silly, they can become supported by group members.

For example, in a recent teaching exercise a group of students instructed to come up with a group identity called themselves the 'We hate Sean Smythe Group' because the only common identity that they could find (they were put together at random) was a dislike of Sean's teaching. Groups do not always produce a reasonable average of individual's attitudes, but instead can discover agreement, with each person then using that to support their adopting a more extreme position than they began with.

Risky shift

As well as attitudes, groups also tend to make more extreme decisions than individuals. The opposite, perhaps more common-sense, view of groups was popular among social psychologists until Stoner (1961) demonstrated that groups did not simply reach balanced, cautious decisions, but were inclined to make decisions that involved more risk than those made by individuals on their own. The dominant attitude in the group became exaggerated in the individual members so that a more extreme group decision was reached. This phenomenon has become known as the 'risky shift'.

Stoner's experiments were conducted using management students from Massachusetts Institute of Technology. In his first study individuals were presented with dilemmas and asked to consider them privately. The individuals were then formed into groups of six and were presented with the same dilemmas. They were instructed that they had to make a unanimous choice and give a range of cautious and risky outcomes to decide upon. The typical group decision was riskier than the average of the individuals' previous decisions.

Several studies have since replicated the results of this initial study. Using different methods for example, Kogan and Wallach (1964) posed life situation problems involving a central person with a choice between more or less risky courses of actions. For each situation, the subject's task was to choose the lowest likelihood of success that s/he would accept before recommending the alternative of higher risk. The riskiest decision was rated 1 in 10 and the most conservative decision was 9 in 10. Individuals were first asked to fill in the option choices, then discuss them in a group setting to reach a consensus. After group discussion, individuals then filled in the option choices again. The findings showed that the decision made by the group after a period of discussion was more risky than the average individual decisions made before discussion by the group members. This seemed to be regardless of gender of subjects or group size.

Another example of attitude shift in real life is from an American study carried out at Bennington College for women. The political ethos there had always been predominantly liberal – what would be called left wing in Europe – and it was discovered that the longer the students stayed at the college the more liberal their attitudes became.

Group polarisation

As more research was conducted on group decision-making, it was clear that other kinds of attitudinal shift could occur. Stoner also noted a shift to caution, whereby the group would arrive at a more cautious decision compared to the average of the individual opinion. Moscovici and Zavalloni (1969) write of *group polarisation* in that the group becomes a polariser of attitudes, rather than always leading to a more risky shift. In other words, the group decision will be more extreme than that expressed by the average of the individuals' decisions but will tend to shift in the same direction.

Moscovici and Zavalloni (1969) demonstrated polarisation in a study that measured the attitudes to President de Gaulle in individual French high school pupils and compared them to their attitudes to Americans. This was followed by a discussion on each topic and the pupils then had to reach an agreement on their attitudes. Not too surprisingly – pre 1968 – the individuals' attitudes towards de Gaulle were for the most part highly favourable, while those towards Americans were moderately unfavourable. However, what is more interesting is that after group discussion the agreed attitude was even more favourable to de Gaulle and even less favourable to Americans. This is a clear demonstration of group polarisation, in that the group tends to shift along the originally favoured pole (if it is positive then it becomes more positive and if it is negative then it becomes more negative). It can be seen then that this phenomenon is not just related to risk factors but also to attitudes; this study illustrates how the attitudes of the group become more extreme than those previously expressed by individuals.

Such studies may be criticised based on the artificiality of the experimental situation. Therefore, a question that you may be asking yourself is 'do phenomena such as polarisation and risky shift apply in "natural" groups as opposed to "experimental" groups?' In natural groups members are more likely to know each other and have existing social relationships, rather than being chosen randomly, as experimental groups tend to be. Decisions will be acted on and will therefore have consequences for the individual members involved as well as others.

However, studies of real decision-making groups including university examiners, medical teams, student union committees and judges, tend to still find polarisation, although not always in such extreme form (Fraser *et al.*, 1971). Polarisation of attitudes in groups also occurs when no decisions are involved (as with the study of French students mentioned above). Whilst group polarisation does occur in many cases, it is not inevitable. It may depend on many aspects of the group including its structure, communication and leadership. As we will see shortly, real-life groups are capable of making terrible decisions with disastrous consequences.

Groupthink

Irvine Janis (1972) coined the term 'groupthink' to describe an extreme example of group polarisation or in other words the extreme attitudes and decisions of a cohesive group. Janis defined 'groupthink' as:

> A determination of mental efficiency, reality testing and moral judgement that results from in-group pressures.

His book describes many instances of military and political decision-making which showed utmost stupidity despite the high intelligence of group members. One commonly cited example was the Bay of Pigs fiasco in 1961. This was when President Kennedy and his small group of advisors made a disastrous decision to send a relatively small group of Cuban exiles to invade the Cuban coast with the support of the US Airforce. The invasion was intended to overthrow Fidel Castro but everything went hopelessly wrong, and the invaders were either killed or captured. Objectively, it seems inconceivable that despite the high intelligence of Kennedy and his group of advisors, they believed that a relatively ill-equipped and small group of Cuban exiles would be able to land on Cuba, get past a well-equipped and vigilant Cuban army, prompt the local community to revolt, and seize control of the island. Kennedy and his advisors later admitted it was a stupid move. The principles of 'groupthink' outlined below can help explain how this fiasco happened in the first place.

Further examples of 'groupthink' can be observed in other examples of military catastrophes including accounts of the battles of Pearl Harbor and of Arnhem (for further reading see Janis, 1982). Business examples that have been analysed in this way include the Maxwell Corporation and the Barings Bank collapse (Brotherton, 1999: 81–5). As we write, we cannot help wondering if British involvement in the bombing campaign in Kosovo/Yugoslavia was decided by 'groupthink'. Only time will tell, but the reader may like to consider which of the following characteristics seem to describe the current (2000) British New Labour Government.

The essential characteristics of 'groupthink' (for more detail see Janis, 1982) are:

1　The members belong to a cohesive group.
2　The group members often share very similar backgrounds and attitudes to each other and to their leader (and the effect can be greater if there is a strong, autocratic, leader).

3 The decision process is strongly oriented towards consensus, leading to one-sided and incorrect conclusions.
4 The group develops an 'illusion of invulnerability' coupled with extreme optimism: 'If we all work together on this we won't go wrong.'
5 The group overestimates its own morality: 'We are doing this for the good of everyone.'
6 The group ignores inconvenient ethical issues and rationalises blind spots.
7 The group stereotypes out groups, perceiving them as weak, evil, or stupid.
8 The group adopts a fixed and uncritical mode of thinking: 'We don't have to go over it again. We have considered all the options and no other option is feasible.'
9 Conformity and suppression of individual doubts occur.
10 The group develops a belief that everyone has voiced their opinion and that the decision is a consensus of divergent views.
11 The group's concern is for an answer at any cost, rather than no answer.
12 Unvoiced doubts lead to an 'illusion of unanimity' in decisions: 'So we have agreed, haven't we, to proceed?'
13 Individual members take on the role of 'mindguards' silencing disagreement from others in the group.
14 The group fails to identify expertise among its members.

To guard against poor decision-making in groups, we should all beware of the above characteristics.

How to avoid 'groupthink'

How then can we avoid 'groupthink' when we are members of a tightly knit group? One good thing about human error is the ability to learn from it. For example, Janis (1982) observed that whilst the Kennedy administration made a disastrous miscalculation in supporting the Bay of Pigs they subsequently used procedures which ensured that important decisions were thoroughly discussed. They even went as far as appointing a 'devil's advocate' at every meeting whereby one member of the group would highlight the negative aspects of every proposal.

Below we have listed five functions of decision-making groups that will help avoid 'groupthink'. These are partly modelled after the five critical functions proposed by Hirokawa's work (1988) on group communication and decision-making as well as considering some important points made by Sutherland (1992: 67).

1 Careful discussion of the problem.
2 Clarify objectives.
3 Careful examination of criteria for successful outcome.
4 Consider alternative courses of action.
5 Provide reasons for and against each proposal.

Another point worth considering is that the group should take breaks from the task. This disturbs the cohesion of the group and may give individuals time to reconsider. Decision-making groups that are fulfilling the above criteria have the best chances of success. In addition, there are some things that you can do personally to combat 'groupthink':

6 Avoid ignoring important facts irrespective of how annoying or inconvenient they seem.
7 Avoid endorsing stereotypical views of the opposition or people outside the group.
8 Avoid resisting the urge to suppress your own doubts – speak up!
9 Avoid the urge to please or agree with the leader for your own personal benefit or simply out of conformity.

In fairness, it must be said that in some organisations resisting 'groupthink' can be personally dangerous – the Maxwell Organisation having been one such example. However, it is always worth considering carefully the extent to which the groups you are involved in *really* punish nonconformity and disobedience. If this is widely believed in your organisation, what is the evidence? We will also emphasise further in Chapter 11 the need to promote methods of group working that discourage 'groupthink' and facilitate flexible and creative approaches to problems.

Having looked at the kinds of problem that can occur in group decisions, we will now turn to consider the causes of these problems in further detail, with an emphasis on less dramatic problems than those created by 'groupthink'. We will discuss these under the two headings of decision-making processes and group processes, but there is considerable overlap.

Decision-making processes

Usually, a group has a problem to solve and there is a range of solutions, some already known, others not known. If the solution is clear and everyone agrees on it, then there will be no difficulty stating the group's conclusions. Often the group has a lot of information, but the information is confusing and incomplete and no amount of discussion will reveal what would actually happen if a particular solution were adopted. In short, it is common for groups to be searching for certainties when none are really available and this may lead them to grasp offers that are socially appealing, but may not be sensible.

Agree whatever someone fancies

Sometimes, a group will go along quite quickly with any decision that somebody is strongly in favour of, and fail to consider alternatives. The person who proposes the solution can take the agreement of others to be evidence that the solution is correct, when alone she might have thought more about alternatives. The rest of the group mistakenly assume that the proposer has thought through her suggested solution carefully. In consequence, everybody incorrectly imagines that enough thought has been given to achieve a good outcome.

For example, a purchasing committee member may strongly favour a new computer system; they lack the expertise to assess it, but liked the sales team, their pitch and their hospitality. At the purchasing committee meeting, nobody has strong feelings; they have to use up the relevant budget, so the system is purchased. It turns out to have major flaws that make it almost unusable. This scenario occurred quite often in the National Health Service in the late 1980s.

Consensus at any cost

Sometimes, each time one of the obvious solutions is suggested, someone is strongly opposed to it. Eventually, someone suggests an alternative that no one opposes vigorously, and which may then be adopted even though it is not sensible. Such alternatives can sometimes be quite strange, even obviously stupid when looked at carefully, but the group is so pleased it reached a solution that they did not take the time to look at it carefully.

For example, a committee was meeting to discuss the problem of laboratory teaching space, which was unsuitable for computer use. The obvious solutions were to refurbish the existing laboratories, or to build new ones. Both had strong opponents and strong advocates. After a long debate, somebody suggested cutting 4 cm off the legs of the existing laboratory stools, which did not make the laboratories suitable for computer use. Nonetheless, this decision was implemented.

Unworkable compromises

Another thing that can happen is that if different people favour different solutions, someone else suggests a compromise solution that contains elements of both. The group can be so pleased with the compromise that again they fail to think through its consequences. It might have been better to adopt one of the solutions that some liked and others did not.

For example, most public organisations now use staff appraisal. Trade unions were generally opposed to appraisal. As a compromise, in some organisations compulsory appraisal procedures have been set up, but kept separate from promotion procedures. What, then, is the point of appraisal? At minimum, having two sets of procedures wastes effort and is probably unfair.

An agreed solution does not guarantee a workable solution

Yet another thing that can go wrong is that the group fail to realise that they have not collected enough information to make a rational decision, or fail to recognise an obvious flaw in the decision that they have reached. Where an individual might get others to check information, or decisions, a group may think that as they all agree, at that point, no further checking is required. An unwise, risky, or dangerous plan may be implemented. Baruch Fischhoff (see Sutherland, 1992: 236) has shown that people (individuals and groups) find it difficult to defer forming opinions or making decisions until enough information is available.

Responsibility is diffused

A final phenomenon that can contribute to poor decision-making is that individuals can avoid taking individual responsibility for decisions. Collective responsibility can provide social support for hard decisions: 'The committee decided to make him redundant.' However, this can sometimes turn to collective irresponsibility, where nobody takes responsibility for poor or unpopular decisions: 'The management has decided to make you redundant.' But exactly who are 'the management'? If nobody has to take responsibility for decisions then there is less pressure to make good decisions. Diffusion of responsibility is discussed again below.

SWOT analysis

The processes of group decision-making involve discussion and discussion can cloud and conceal problems as well as solving them. One way around this can be to conduct some form of cost-benefit analysis, such as SWOT analysis that attempts to list and evaluate the implications of alternatives. SWOT stands for Strengths, Weaknesses, Opportunities, Threats: in this approach the group, or indeed an individual, is encouraged to list and consider these features for each solution that is discussed. *Strengths* are the good and positive features of the solution. *Weaknesses* are the bad and negative features. *Opportunities* are the benefits that the solution might bring, which are less definite than strengths. *Threats* are the dangers that the solution raises, especially if it goes wrong; again these are less definite than weaknesses. SWOT analysis cannot produce 'the right solution', but it encourages systematic thinking about the decision to be made and usually identifies areas where more information should be obtained. Basically, this approach takes the procedures for avoiding 'groupthink' one step further.

Example: SWOT analysis of buying a house

Strengths

> We like the house.
>
> We want somewhere nice to live.
>
> It is a good neighbourhood.
>
> We do not have enough space where we live now. This house is bigger.

Weaknesses

> It costs a lot of money.
>
> The move will involve a lot of upheaval and stress.
>
> We will leave behind the familiar neighbourhood.

Opportunities

> The children will be able to go to a better school.

We will have a better standard of life.

It is an easier commute to work.

Threats

What if we cannot pay the mortgage?

If we need to move elsewhere for work, will we be able to sell it easily?

There is talk of the company relocating to new premises on the other side of town that might mean a long commute.

You then take each feature and attempt to assess how important it is. How much do you like the house? Is it a unique house of a kind that is hard to find, or are there many other houses like it? How likely is the company relocation? To evaluate the features it may well be worth finding out more information, but there are no certainties. For all you know the children may hate their new school, however good it looks. You can also do SWOT analysis when there is more than one solution – perhaps you are trying to decide between two different houses.

Group processes

Seeking approval

As we have seen in preceding chapters group acceptance and approval is very important for individual members. If the prevailing group attitude appears to be going in one direction, then individual members may suppress contrary attitudes so as not to lose the approval of the group, although it has been shown that exposure to minority views can improve group decision-making. Group members may also express more extreme forms of group attitudes in order to win approval. Both processes can tend to escalate, as more extreme expressions exaggerate perceived group norms for other members. A state may be reached where group members are all publicly expressing quite extreme attitudes, while suppressing private reservations about what they are saying and assuming that other group members actually endorse the attitudes being expressed.

For example, in ghetto gangs, group pressures encourage the expression of extreme verbal and physical aggression towards rival gangs. The most extreme and violent gang members are often younger members who wish to be accepted into the gang. Older members may actually take a more pragmatic view of rivalries, but cannot easily express moderate views without losing status.

Such tendencies are present in much moderated form in many commercial activities. Two managing directors of rival firms may well play golf together and informally share selected business information, while not admitting this to their subordinates and while encouraging their subordinates to take an unrealistically negative view of their rival's products. Some of the sales team may realise that their home improvement product is almost identical to their rival's – they will tend to keep such thoughts quiet at work; others may actually believe in the superiority of their product – they will tend to exaggerate this as a result of group processes.

Conviction and conformity

The finding that individuals are prepared to take more risks in group decision-making is influenced by the amount of conviction that the members have in the group. Studies have shown that individual members trust the accuracy of the group's decisions more than those made by themselves. This is perhaps another case of conformity.

Normative effect

People tend to regard their own views as less extreme and more normal than others. In groups, people with extreme views can pull the 'norm' in their direction, as others compare themselves favourably with the more extreme views and come to believe that their own views are moderate.

Diffusion of responsibility

Diffusion of responsibility is another important factor. Each member of the group feels less personal responsibility for the decision and is able to both advocate more risk and engage in more extreme behaviours that they perceive to be group norms. Zimbardo (1969) has referred to this as de-individuation. For example, in gangs responsibility is diffused and acts are committed in a group that would be unthinkable by people on their own.

Informational effect

Groups tend to focus too much on discussing what is positive and pleasant about their decisions, and not enough about what is negative and bad. People who are critical of favoured decisions and plans may be regarded as disloyal, or personally critical of group members. They may even be formally or informally excluded from the group (or even hung for mutiny! see Sobel, 1996: Ch. 1). In fact, as we will see in Chapter 11 on teams, being critical is an important role in a group.

Living with decisions

This can be as important as making them in the first place. It is worth re-emphasising that few group (or individual) decisions can be made based on complete information, with certainty. A notice we have seen in a number of computer rooms reads:

'You can have information that is
- Cheap
- Accurate
- Quick

pick any two.'

The same may be said for decisions. In consequence, decisions are often fallible. One suggested rule of management (we do not know of any empirical evidence to back it up) is that when managers dele-gate decisions they should support the staff who made them, even when they turn out to be wrong, as long as the staff and the organ-isation learn from the mistakes. The Kennedy administration certainly learned from the Bay of Pigs.

It is extremely easy to live with a decision if you agreed with it all along and its results are good. Problems occur when you do not agree with it, or when the results are bad. One problem here is the wisdom of hindsight. Once they know the outcome of a decision people tend to think that they 'knew that all along'. People therefore tend to be biased against the people who made a poor decision, because they think that they would have done better. This is largely a delusion based on hindsight. One aspect of living with decisions is to be forgiving when they go wrong.

Another aspect is to enact the decision, once it is made. All too often, a group reaches a decision, but various individuals who disagree do their best to prevent the decision being enacted. This simply wastes time and often it is better to have a decision, even if it is not the best one, rather than no decision. For example, if your company cannot buy any computers until the purchasing committee chooses the supplier and no computers are available meantime, then perhaps a quick decision is more important than choosing the very best system.

The third aspect of living with decisions is probably most important of all: to learn from decisions and use their results to feedback into improving the decision-making process. Generally speaking, progress is made possible by learning from mistakes. In many work environments mistakes are punished, or widely believed to be punished. In consequence, mistakes are covered-up as far as possible and no corporate learning occurs. There are several ways of covering up mistaken decisions:

- Deny responsibility for the decision (or blame someone else).
- Conceal or deny all evidence that the decision was a mistake, but continue with the line of action despite its costs or lack of success ('groupthink' can contribute to this).
- Quietly drop the decision and suppress further discussion (easiest if you are relatively powerful).
- Reverse the decision, but insist that there has been no such reversal. Remember how the phrase 'This lady's not for turning' came back to haunt Margaret Thatcher as she had to reverse a number of important policy decisions including the 'poll tax'.

Tempting as they can be, do not do these things because they hinder progress.

Conclusions

This chapter has looked at the ways in which group decisions can be defective and suggested some remedies for these defects. It has also looked at groups where different interests are represented and the problems that can arise there. Group decisions and group working are based on complex and fallible processes. We have identified only some of the general difficulties that can arise. The essential things are to be sensitive to group processes, to be aware of how these can distort decision-making and to be willing to try to improve things.

Exercise

Running a committee

You have been asked to head your department's new planning committee.

- How will you ensure that different views are represented?
- As the chair of the committee how will you deal with people who try to flatter you?
- When people on the committee express negative views of other departments, how will you deal with this?
- How would you run your committee meetings to ensure that group polarisation did not occur?

Recommended reading

Brotherton, C. (1999) *Social Psychology and Management*, Milton Keynes: Open University Press.

Janis, I. (1982) *Victims of Groupthink: A Psychological Study of Foreign Policy Decisions and Fiascos*, second edition, Boston, MA: Houghton Mifflin.

Janis, I.L. and Mann, L. (1977) *Decision Making*, New York: Free Press.

Steiner, I.D. (1972) *Group Processes and Productivity*, New York: Academic Press.

Sutherland, S. (1992) *Irrationality*, London: Penguin.

10 Working beyond the group

In most organisations, many groups meet to represent a range of departments, groups or interests. Meetings also commonly occur across company or organisational boundaries and this style of networked working is becoming more common. The Labour Government has coined the phrase 'Joined-up government' for example. Under such conditions, it is not enough to consider the group as a single group of people with a common purpose. Many groups – including those discussed in the previous chapter – are groups of representatives of other groups. Indeed, group members often feel conflicting loyalties between the current group and the group that they are supposed to represent. What if the 'best' decision for the current group's purpose has a poor outcome for the people that they represent? This chapter will look at some of the processes involved when interests beyond a single group are concerned.

In Chapter 9 we considered decision-making within groups and the influence of groups on individuals. In work settings we are often concerned with relationships between groups, for example, relationships between management and shop floor staff. Studies on intergroup relationships are the basis of 'employee relations'. There are two basic approaches: the study of negotiation and bargaining and the study of conflict and its reduction. We will focus on group mechanisms that occur when the group is composed of people representing different interests, rather than being a cohesive group of the kind already described.

Objectives

By the end of this chapter you should

- Know the main methods of negotiation and conflict resolution.
- Be aware of some of the problems and difficulties that can arise.

- Know some of the types of barrier that can arise for inter-agency working.

Negotiating groups

Power is perhaps the most obvious way to settle conflict. In a hierarchical structure, power is often used to dominate discussion and resolve differences by imposing a solution. The advantage is that answers can be found quickly. The main disadvantage is that an imposed solution will cause resentment in anybody who perceives the solution to be a loss for them. Resentment may lead to difficulties in implementing the decision and to problems later, when people's co-operation is required. It is not good policy to always win at work, even if you have the power to do so, if winning involves others losing. The ideal solution is a 'win-win' solution where nobody feels that they have lost. Imposed solutions are also particularly subject to the problems of 'groupthink'.

Negotiation is preferable to dominance and in most organisations and networks compromises are necessary. However, there are some obvious disadvantages. Negotiation can occupy valuable time and hence miss other opportunities. Some parties may negotiate insincerely. Bargaining may seem like a sign of weakness to some, which could result in low levels of commitment to the final decisions made. Nonetheless, it is hard to see how large organisations could function without some level of negotiating and bargaining. Much of this activity occurs within a group setting, where different group members represent different interests. For example, different sections of an organisation may send representatives to a committee where research and development funds are allocated for the year. Representatives have both to sell their section's bid and to judge other bids.

There are two extreme forms of such a group. At one extreme there may be a totally confrontational meeting between two or more 'teams' who feel that they have little or nothing in common and whose aim is to get the best deal possible for their side. There may also be neutral mediators or facilitators, although their 'neutrality' may be suspected by at least one side. Old-fashioned 1960s negotiations between trade unions and management could be like this.

The other extreme form of such a group is that it actually becomes a cohesive group that makes joint decisions. Group members come to feel more affinity with the group than with the people that they are supposed to represent there. While this can lead to easier decision-making (subject to the problems described above), members may fail to serve adequately as representatives of the people or group that sent them to the meeting. Often the public face of such groups is more confrontational than the private discussions. Among the signs that negotiations may have become cosy like this is that group members 'swap sides' when moving job. For example, a few years ago the administrative head of the AUT (Association of University Teachers) moved to an important job for the main national university management group.

Most negotiating groups lie somewhere between these two extremes and most people sent to negotiate on behalf of others to a group will feel somewhat divided in their loyalties. The most common form of this is when managers of different teams, sections or departments meet to decide common policies and resource allocations. Each manager has to represent their department's interests while also making (or accepting, in more autocratic organisations) collective decisions and bringing them back to the department.

Unless such a negotiating group can come to operate effectively as a group, or team, it is unlikely to be able to reach effective or sensible decisions. Instead it is likely to reach 'decisions' that simply represent the interests of the most powerful parties present, make ineffective decisions the only merit of which is to offend nobody, or make no decisions at all because agreement is always impossible. What makes a group or team effective is discussed elsewhere in this book.

Special issues for negotiating

Insincere reasons for negotiation

As with any group decision-making, or any teamwork, it is essential that everyone involved in negotiations shares agreed goals – most obviously that some solution is reached. Parties can agree to be involved in negotiations for other reasons, which will often prevent a solution being reached:

- Because they have no choice.
- In order to stall to gain an advantage. They may know that their bargaining position will improve with time, or that the problem or issue being discussed will disappear.
- In the hope that once negotiations get nowhere, the status quo will be retained. Negotiations may even be actively disrupted to this end.
- In order to reach an unworkable solution that will discredit those who try to implement it, to the manipulative party's advantage.

- Because taking part in the negotiations is a cover for other decision-making activities that are going on elsewhere. They may have made a secret deal that will be implemented once the 'democratic' negotiations have broken down.

The need for agreed goals or objectives

It is helpful if, from the outset, different parties are clear about what they would like, what they would be content with and what they could bear. Negotiations can get nowhere if one or more parties 'Don't know what they want and won't be happy until they get it.' This is all too common and can lead to every suggestion being rejected.

Perhaps to state the obvious, negotiation usually involves compromise. This can mean reaching a compromise position on a point, or each side getting their way on some points, in some kind of balanced way. If one or more parties is unwilling to compromise then negotiations are unlikely to get anywhere. It will also cause problems if one or more parties compromise insincerely, but do not implement the compromise in practice.

It is important, as far as possible, that the eventual solution can be presented as a 'win-win' solution that will make all parties feel that they have achieved something. It is widely believed that the peace settlement imposed on Germany at the end of the First World War, which Germans generally perceived as both defeat and humiliation, contributed to the rise of the Nazis and the Second World War. Losers tend to want revenge later, or to end up resenting the winners and may try to sabotage decisions they feel were forced upon them. Even when groups have agreed a compromise, one or more parties may feel resentful about it. Such feelings are better acknowledged and discussed within the group than simply left to fester.

The time factor in negotiations

Hasty decisions can often be bad decisions, but lengthy negotiations can cause a number of problems that should be considered.

The decision-making situation will tend to change with time and an initial solution can become irrelevant or lose its competitive advantage while the fine details are being worked out to everybody's satisfaction. Some decisions need to be made quickly for this reason alone and in some situations any decision is better than excessive delay. For example, should one product be developed or another? There will be an element of risk attached to both, but assuming that both are reasonably researched products, developing either one is preferable to developing neither while discussions continue.

As negotiations drag on, it is likely that much more time has been spent discussing problems and disagreements than in discussing advantages and common ground. This can demotivate everybody and lead to a loss of enthusiasm for the final agreement, which may even be seen as a 'lose-lose' result, where everybody feels that they have compromised excessively, or where the advocates of one solution have been effectively put off it by criticism. One role of neutral arbitration can be to point out repeatedly what all parties agree about. Negotiations where parties really do not agree at all usually break down quite rapidly, or are strung out for the insincere reasons discussed above.

As time passes, people are also likely to change their minds, even if they have not been specifically demotivated by the negotiating process. One useful role in a management team is the 'resource investigator' (Belbin, 1996) who spends a lot of time interacting outside the team and discovering new ideas. However, this sort of person can also lose enthusiasm for ideas, because they will move on to something else new. Powerful resource investigators in an organisation can push forward the new briefly, to cancel it when the newer arrives. This can waste resources and prevent the implementation of any coherent plans. People sometimes completely change their minds, but they more often wax and wane in their enthusiasm. With time, somebody who was extremely enthusiastic about something is likely to become less so; that is the only way their attitudes could shift.

With more time, it also becomes possible to gather too much information, identify too many difficulties with any decision or project and endlessly broaden the scope of the negotiations. If the decision to be negotiated has become so complex that nobody really understands what is involved, then there is a need to cut back upon what is being decided and defer or delegate the details. There may also be issues about the format of the information, which perhaps should be provided in briefer and clearer ways. As described in Chapter 8, information can be one source of personal power and people sometimes present information in difficult ways on purpose, to impress colleagues and make themselves appear indispensable.

Methods of dealing with conflict

When conflict occurs there are four appropriate responses that are possible. You can:

- Defer to the other party and let them have their way.
- Negotiate and reach a compromise with the other party that satisfies both equally, if not fully.
- Compete with the other party and attempt to win.
- Co-operate with the other party to achieve a mutually agreeable win-win solution.

There are, of course, also inappropriate responses. Common ones are:

- Avoiding the conflict, usually by avoiding the other party or putting off conflict resolution.
- Direct 'all out' aggression to force the other party to back down. At work this is usually only verbal aggression, but it involves attacking the party by any means, including insults and bringing up old grievances, not just addressing, or competing, over the specific conflict.
- Working past the other party, by pretending to resolve the conflict while doing whatever you want without their knowledge.
- Withdrawal of co-operation, so that conflict resolution has to occur without your consent and you 'reserve the right' to dislike the outcome.
- Manipulative emotionality, such as endless complaining – whining one would say in children – or getting hysterical, that forces others to concede to you.

Few people never do any of these things, but, as all parents know in the case of children, they can be extremely frustrating to deal with. Fortunately, it is usually individuals, rather than entire teams that misbehave in these ways. It can be helpful to realise that people are not necessarily misbehaving on purpose, but have usually learned to get their own way by these means in the past. It is also helpful to realise that misbehaviour is often triggered when a person feels under threat and the conflict may threaten them. To deal with inappropriate methods of conflict it is important to:

- Not give in to the behaviour.
- Not respond in kind, which will escalate the problem.
- Point out that you do not like the person's behaviour.
- Offer to reschedule a time to resolve the conflict when they have calmed down.
- Try to use an appropriate method of conflict yourself, as this minimises the likelihood of people feeling threatened.

Choosing the most appropriate method of conflict

The following guidelines (Adler and Towne, 1993: 399) were developed for interpersonal communication, but they apply also to group negotiations.

Consider deferring:

- When you discover that you are wrong. One aspect of a well-functioning group is that people can admit that they are wrong.
- When the issue is more important to the other party than it is to your party.
- To let others learn by making their own mistakes.
- When the long-term cost of winning may not be worth the short-term gains. A special case of this at work is when the other party is considerably more powerful than you and liable to wield that power against you.

Consider compromising:

- When there is not enough time to seek a win-win outcome.
- When the issue is not important enough to negotiate at length.
- When the other parties are not willing to seek a win-win outcome.

Consider competing:

- When the issue is important and the other parties will take advantage of your non-competitive approach.

Consider co-operating:

- When the issue is too important for a compromise.
- When the long-term relationship between the parties is important.
- When the other parties are willing to co-operate.

Summary of negotiation

Negotiating requires that negotiators can work sincerely together towards agreed goals, while continuing to represent those that they are supposed to represent. Solutions usually require compromise and are easier if parties are clear what they want, willing to accept compromise and able to present the solution as a success rather than a failure.

Negotiations that take too long can cause problems, as can inappropriate responses to conflict.

Multi-agency working

Working across groups can occur when different agencies, or different teams within the same organisation, are required to co-operate on some project. Many of the difficulties already described will tend to occur. For, at minimum, such work will require that different agencies negotiate their roles and contributions, and often a common budget as well.

'Joined-up government'

A major extension of inter-agency working in Britain has recently seen a number of governmental initiatives, including Drug Action Teams and Youth Justice Teams, that require different local agencies to work together and to provide a common pool of funds for various purposes. These agencies commonly include the police, criminal justice workers – such as probation officers and youth justice workers – social workers, health service workers and educationalists. They usually bring with them very different skills and approaches to problems.

Variations in work cultures

Work cultures can differ in a number of ways that it is important to recognise in inter-agency working.

Meaning

The meanings of words and the use of language can differ in important ways. For example, many people have 'supervision' at work but the nature of this relationship with a manager can be extremely varied. In some jobs supervision simply involves giving orders; in others, supervision is about the personal development of the employee; in some supervision is more about quality control and checking work; and in others again 'the supervisor' is a more experienced person who makes the unusual and more difficult decisions. This can lead to confusion when provisions for 'supervision' in an inter-agency team are being discussed.

Another example is that when technicians and sales staff talk about 'the product' they will usually be referring to the same physical objects, but have very different understandings of 'the product'. This may cause problems; sales staff may see the product as something that satisfies customer demand, while technical staff see it as something that can be achieved with current engineering methods. For example, Apple Computers struggled in the early 1990s in part because they developed a confusing variety of products on the basis of what could be engineered without enough consideration of sales. More recently, the Apple Imac comes in several colours (among other innovations) and has sold very well, although engineers are unlikely to care what colour a computer is. On the other hand an attractive product from the sales point of view, such as a smaller 4-wheel drive vehicle, may be problematic from the engineering point of view; some tended to fall over when cornering.

Working practices

Expectations about working practices and organisation vary enormously. For instance, different levels of formality may be expected by different agencies, so that one kind of staff finds the other excessively formal, the other finds the first inappropriately informal. Some staff may be used to 'watching the clock', while others are used to autonomy. The supervision and management of one agency's staff by others may cause problems because expectations differ so much.

One example is that university staff tend not to keep regular hours, are accustomed to working to long deadlines, but producing work of very high quality, and to an annual work cycle that revolves around the university year. Civil servants tend to keep regular hours, work to short deadlines producing work of pragmatic quality and work steadily year-round except for statutory holidays. When university staff are asked to bid for research work for the government, the deadlines can seem unrealistically short to them and the timing of bids can be inconvenient relative to the academic year.

When inter-agency working occurs, there is always a risk that different agencies are judged by inappropriate standards, rather than being appreciated for their worth and contribution. There can also be pressures that encourage staff to try to live up to inappropriate standards, so academics may come to work as mediocre civil servants, rather than making a useful contribution as academic researchers, for example.

Conditions of work

Pay and working conditions may also be very different. When different team members come from different professions then they may be paid very differently. For example, community psychiatric teams often contain psychiatrists, clinical psychologists and psychiatric nurses. The nurses tend to earn less than £30,000, the psychologists up to about £45,000 and the psychiatrists often earn more than £50,000 and can earn three times that. It is not surprising that this can cause some resentment; it *is* surprising that this does not appear to be a major problem. Differences in working conditions can cause more problems, particularly when this results in some staff having to cover for others. For example, staff from education are often employed and paid on the basis that they take the long school holidays. This is fine if they work in a school, but not if they work with staff from health-care and elsewhere, who do not get these holidays but instead have to cover while the education staff take the summer off.

Organisational structure and procedures

The financial and administrative structures of different organisations will vary. These differences often include different accounting methods, different methods of financial responsibility, different requirements for auditing and monitoring work, different procedures for getting equipment and resources, different computer systems and different expectations about what should happen. A person from one organisation where there is some financial autonomy may simply be able to go out, purchase a minor piece of equipment, such as an answering machine, and take the money from petty cash. In another organisation, this equipment must be purchased centrally from an approved supplier. In one organisation, staff are expected to use computers themselves to look up central records and enter new ones. In another organisation, staff are actively discouraged from this because it is clerical work that can only be done by a few clerical workers who fiercely guard the information. Clearly there will be difficulties when trying to develop joint work across two very different organisations.

Other cultural differences

The culture of different teams and agencies can differ in all sorts of other ways. Some of these can be quite subtle, but nonetheless cause problems. For example, medical doctors tend to defer to their hierarchy. They can be reluctant to disagree openly with more senior colleagues, willing to be authoritarian with juniors, and competitive with equals, whom they interact least with. This approach does not work when they are trying to interact with other professions, who are probably best treated as equals. Instead, some less skilled medics can lurch between awkward silence and patronising outbursts when they are trying to deal with other professions. It is not possible to provide a list of cultural differences, but you should be sensitive to their existence, and the potential for problems.

Improving interagency groups

- Beware of the potential difficulties – these have been described above.
- Use a powerful chair or mediator who can prevent squabbling over resources – this person usually needs to be senior enough to have financial control over some or all of the agencies involved and may, for example, be a senior member of local government, or a senior manager who has responsibility over all the teams or departments involved.
- Provide sufficient financial autonomy – no team or committee can decide anything useful if they have no control over the funds to pay for their actions.
- Explicitly discuss and decide upon working practices – these may need to be entirely new, or based upon existing agency practices.
- Encourage flexibility amongst staff.

There will be difficulties in working as a team with people from very diverse backgrounds. These difficulties can be overcome if staff are willing to be flexible and to learn from and resolve problems. It is useful to ensure that staff's main loyalties move to the group or team and are not kept with their parent agencies. The best way of achieving this is to avoid seconding staff on a short-term or part-time basis and to avoid as far as possible keeping their line management at the parent agency.

Conclusions

If working effectively in groups is complex, working effectively in a group representing different interests is even more difficult, because there can be conflicts between different interests and variations in the cultures of different organisations, or of groups within the same organisation. In Chapter 11 we will look in more detail at the construction of workplace teams, before going on to look at networking in Chapter 12.

Exercises

Stating a negotiating position

As the representative of the section of the organisation you work for you have been invited to a committee to discuss the allocation of funds for staff training and development for the year. Up until now your section has always received less funds for staff training than any other section. Your section is eager for this not to occur this year. How will you sell your section's bid? How do you intend to deal with conflict from opposing parties? What sort of compromise, if any, would you be willing to accept as the negotiator for your section?

Avoiding Attack

Conflicts often get worse because people attack each other. List some strategies to avoid attacking colleagues who are aggressive in meetings when things are not going their way and who rebuff your proposals. Hint: consider assertive responding, dealing with emotionality, as well as styles of negotiation.

Cultural differences

Take two organisations that you have worked for, or are familiar with. What are the main cultural differences between these two organisations? Try to cover all the main factors mentioned in that section. Do these differences have major effects on methods of working?

Recommended reading

Adler, R.B. and Towne, N. (1993) *Looking Out / Looking In*, seventh edition, Fort Worth: Harcourt Brace Jovanovich.
Belbin, R.M. (1996) *Management Teams – Why They Succeed or Fail*, Woburn: Butterworth–Heinemann.

11 Teams and roles

> Teams will be the primary building blocks of the organisation of
> the future.
>
> (Katzenbach and Smith, 1993)

The aim of this chapter is to look at a particular sort of social group
– teams. We examine the various aspects of teams including team
roles and team building and the communication networks utilised.
We also examine some of the methods of getting teams in organisations
to work most effectively.

Objectives

By the end of this chapter you should be able to:

- Provide a clear definition of a team.
- Understand the various roles in a team.
- Be aware of the importance of teams and team building.
- Illustrate some knowledge of how to get teams to work effectively.
- Understand some of the reasons that teams and groups can be
  dysfunctional.
- Appreciate some of the disadvantages of team work.

What is a team?

If a social group is a collection of people with some sort of purpose,
then a team is a social group with explicit goals that is organised so
that different people's abilities complement each other and produce
a team who perform at their best in achieving their goals.

'Team' can also be used as hollow jargon. In the mid-1990s satirical
TV show *Drop the Dead Donkey* Gus constantly calls the newsroom staff

'Team' and exhorts them to 'Fly the flag of success', and other such clichés. It is fashionable to refer to 'Teams' in the workplace whether the group of people working comprise a team or not. Gus's group of bickering misfits were clearly not a team at all. As we all know, most of the work of the world is done by groups of people whose interactions fall far short of the shiny ideal that Gus pretended to believe in.

So if the label is not enough, then what is a more suitable definition of a team? 'Team' was originally used to refer to a team of animals, usually pulling something. It is important that the team all pull in the same direction and in a co-ordinated manner. A more recent and attractive metaphor is the sports team; a team of people working towards recognised common goals. In a sports team there are recognised roles and clear common goals that, because of the rules of the sport if nothing else, cannot be accomplished alone.

Work is rarely like this. For a start, even if your organisation has a rule book, the competition is not obliged to use the same rules. The required roles in a workplace team may change quite rapidly. As with groups in general, it is helpful if the team has recognised common goals. These goals are not always explained to new group or team members, or are presented in a very abstract way that makes it unclear what members are supposed to do.

Richard still remembers his first game of rugby, taught by a games master who believed that the objectives and rules of rugby if not hereditary, had been firmly instilled in all boys as old as eight. Arriving on the field, he was dimly aware that Rugby was a boy's school and also a game played by something called the 'All Blacks'. One objective seemed to be to move the ball down the field in order to 'score' – whatever that was. However key objectives, such as 'avoid being tackled' and 'identify the opposition team members' escaped him. Having caught the ball by accident he passed it to the first boy who seemed to want it, who unfortunately was on the other team. Many people's first weeks at work are similar. If Richard's first rugby team was a team then he was not yet a part of it.

Modern life is full of lots of things called teams such as Telephone Sales Teams; Management Teams; Quality Assurance Teams; Food Services Teams; Surgical Teams; Social Work Teams; Community Psychiatric Teams; Drug Action Teams. All of these, or the many other groups called teams, lose their right to be called teams if they don't interact properly, or share common goals. Many work groups which would resent being renamed teams may well function as teams. From here on, we will be using 'team' in a technical sense, to refer to a workplace group with certain positive characteristics.

So what is a team? A team is a group of people at work who:

- Work together regularly towards agreed common goals.
- While in the team, regard their team identity as a main feature of their workplace identity.
- Who have largely open communication among themselves.
- Are in the team because of their individual characteristics, although some teams are formed out of whoever is available.
- Who usually adopt a variety of different roles within the team.

Nature of teams

As with group development there is also a growing emphasis on the importance of team building and team development in the workplace. This is particularly the case in large businesses and commercial organisations, where more and more people consider effective teamwork to be the thing of the future. Hence the move towards a greater emphasis on teamwork in the workplace, although there has recently been a backlash questioning whether teams actually work in practice. Our view is that teams are hard to build and easy to damage. The failure of teams to deliver reflects these difficulties, but the ideal of the effective team is still worth working towards. By this stage in this book you should appreciate that we have to work in groups whether we like it or not and there is no real alternative to trying to develop effective workplace groups. A team is an effectively-functioning group.

Permanence of teams

Teams may be formed for particular tasks, disbanding when the task is over. Some companies encourage this sort of flexibility; well-known examples include W. L. Gore (manufacturers of Gortex) and Microsoft. Or teams may be permanent and work on a number of tasks of different kinds over the years. Long-established teams may come to get along extremely well and work effectively together. However, they may also become stale, resistant to change and inward-looking. They may shut out the outside world. Long-established team members may also come to attribute their success to unique personal characteristics. For example, they may regard the charisma of their leader as essential. If key people leave, then the team may no longer function effectively.

Flexible teams, by changing membership and goals regularly, help to prevent these negative characteristics. Their disadvantage is that effective team building can be a lengthy process. Sometimes, the team is just beginning to work really well together when it accomplishes its goals and disbands.

This leads on to another problem. Successful teams may be reluctant to disband. You have probably had the misfortune at one time or another to be forced to work with the colleague or boss from hell (remember one person's hell can be another's heaven). So, most people find it a great relief and pleasure to find themselves getting along with their team and do not want to disband it. The team may even collude, either deliberately or inadvertently, to delay accomplishing the team goals. Surely you all need to check the report just once more then meet again next week!

Team roles

Just as we take on varied roles in the rest of our lives, the roles required in different teams can also vary. Common human resources mistakes are:

- To assume that an employee who is good in one role will be good in another.
- To hire personnel who are 'clones' of the managers doing the hiring, whether suitable for their roles or not.

Teams vary but tend to require a mixture of roles. For example a good committee may include:

- The chair, who is able to welcome all contributions and move business forward.
- People who are enthusiastic for new ideas.
- People who are careful and doubting.
- People who will get the job done, but lack initiative of their own.

Several authors have provided much more specific prescriptions for team members than this. The best known of these is Belbin's (1981) description of team roles, summarised in Table 11.1, and his thesis has also benefited from some empirical support. However, most important is the general idea that a team requires a variety of skills and gains strength from a diversity of people. Many teams have to work with existing staff and the search for the perfect staff list to make up a team may be unrealistic. It is also important to recognise that many people can adopt different team roles, although they will tend to be better in some roles than in others.

Table 11.1 Belbin's team roles

Role	Characteristics	Strengths	Allowable weaknesses
Company worker	Conservative Dutiful Predictable	Good organiser Practical Hard working Self-disciplined	Lack of flexibility Unresponsive to ideas
Chair	Calm Self-confident Controlled	Creating and welcoming contributions Setting objectives	Not an 'ideas' person
Shaper	Highly strung Outgoing Dynamic	Drive Challenges complacency/ineffectiveness/self-deception	Prone to provoke and irritate
Plant	Individualistic Serious-minded Unorthodox	Genius/Imagination/Knowledge	Up in clouds Disregards practical/protocol
Resource investigator	Extroverted Enthusiastic Curious Communicative	Contacting people Exploring the new Responding to challenge	Can lose interest
Monitor evaluator	Sober Unemotional Prudent	Judgement Discretion Hard headed	Lacks inspiration to motivation
Team worker	Socially oriented Mild Sensitive	Responds to team Promotes team spirit	Indecisiveness
Finisher	Painstaking Orderly Anxious Conscientious	Follow-through Perfectionism	Worry Reluctant to let go

Source: Belbin (1981).

Some general implications of this approach:

- People's different personalities affect the ways that they work and what roles they are good at.
- An effective team usually requires a number of different roles – hence people with different traits.
- One should not select 'clones' of existing team members when hiring people, or organising teams.

- It is a bad idea, although comfortable, to work only with people whose temperaments are very like yours.
- In the workplace, people who are sometimes difficult or annoying to others are often making a valuable contribution.

Team building

There has been a great deal of research on the key characteristics of effective teams. Whilst different authors have different views on how effective team development is achieved, there is much overlap in the issues that they believe need to be addressed. Below we describe a group of qualities that we think are essential for a team to work successfully, abstracted from a variety of authors. We would also like to emphasise that among the many existing lists of characteristics cited here you will see at the crux of them is effective communication. If individuals do not communicate with each other effectively in teams then none of the other components will work successfully.

Key attributes of effective teams

Setting the scene

There must be open communication and involvement in discussion about the team purpose, and what objectives and goals need to be fulfilled. As well as clarifying task objectives, a team that is just starting up will have to devote careful consideration to forming issues such as the members' roles and co-ordination.

Ground rules

One way to ensure smooth open communication is to lay down ground rules as soon as the group is formed. If team members already know each other then airing of grievances should also be done at this early stage before the team sets to work. There is no place for resentment and grudges if team unity is to exist, which is an essential component of the fully functional team.

Commitment

A good awareness and understanding of the team approach is beneficial if not essential to the commitment of the team. Open discussion and debate is encouraged.

Smooth interpersonal relationships

Where team members get along without friction or difficulties. A good social climate should be fostered within the team in order to ensure good relationships between team members. Disclosure of feelings is considered here an important feature of successful social relations. Smooth relationships are facilitated by opportunities for normal social interactions, as well as business.

Openness

Values of openness and trust are equally important, where team members feel free to express their thoughts and feelings, both positive and negative. The team should feel able to challenge the status quo with genuine debate about what changes need to be made. Such behaviours should be viewed as beneficial team behaviour.

Shared learning

Where the team share new ideas and approaches aiming for balanced participation as much as possible. The team should be encouraged to admit mistakes, rather than competing with each other.

Good problem-solving and decision-making

Where the team work positively to achieve their goals and avoid shortcuts and jumping to conclusions. Well-defined decision-making procedures are essential for effective teamwork.

Planning both the goals and the process

Proper realistic planning is a crucial component of effective teamwork. It involves setting goals, a realistic time-scale and agreeing methods of operation that are appropriate and workable, including how often the team meets, what it does together and who does what separately elsewhere.

Identified and agreed goals

Teams which lack clearly defined goals will tend to be ineffective, whatever their other merits. Clarity is equally important; team goals must be clear so that everyone knows exactly what is involved. There is little point having clearly defined goals if the team do not understand what is expected of them. Corporate mission statements are often too general to provide clear goals, but they may be useful to steer the goals of specific teams.[1]

Effective leadership

Not all teams have or require a leader. If there is one she or he must be effective.

Ongoing review

Regular team reviews are important in order to ensure that complacency does not set in and that problems are highlighted. It is becoming quite common to have 'away days' where the team goes off somewhere out of the ordinary for the day and reflects on the past and present situation in a more relaxing setting. Regular reviews are also important to encourage teams to openly discuss, in a larger setting, obstacles that they are having difficulty overcoming. Sometimes teams can become 'stuck' but are unsure why this has occurred and/or what to do about it. The use of an external facilitator can often be helpful here.

Sense of purpose

Finally, as well as having clearly defined goals it is useful for a team to have one principal goal from which the smaller goals emerge. It is important that the principal goal (sometimes referred to as a 'mission statement' or a 'team vision') is reviewed regularly in order that it is not forgotten (e.g., Why are we here? What is our main purpose? What is it that we need to achieve?). In order for the principal goal to be effective within the team it must also be clear and precise and inspire motivation and commitment in the team members. It must be realistic and achievable or else the motivation of the team will quickly dissipate. Shared participation in order to develop and attain the goal is important. And finally goals must be able to develop in order to reflect the changes within the group.

Developing a team

Such skills are easy to describe, but hard to do. They require practice and careful implementation. Moreover, it is naive to think that so long as the team is set a challenging goal or exciting task and adheres to the above list of characteristics, then an effective and successful team is sure to emerge. Rather, *practice* is the name of the game. There are essentially two steps:

1   Acquiring knowledge and understanding of the important qualities and skills listed above.
2   Practising the skills; ensuring that they are carefully implemented.

Whilst communication skills are essential for effective teambuilding, it is also a mistake to think that good communication skills alone will produce effective teamwork. If there are clear differences in interest, attitudes or ideas across the team then these may not be easily integrated. The team will have to decide whether they can accept these differences between individual members and still set out to achieve what it is they are together to achieve, or disband before the team becomes dysfunctional. Differences need to be discussed as part of the process of forming a team. Being able to discuss and resolve differences requires open communication, but successfully resolving differences may improve subsequent team openness. See Chapter 10 for more on resolving conflict.

Another possibility for a team is to agree to set aside certain differences between team members as irrelevant to team functioning. It is probably better if these differences can be discussed and then set aside by agreement. Problems seem to arise when differences are not discussed because they are 'supposed to' be irrelevant or unimportant. They may actually be extremely relevant and important for some of the people involved. For instance, modern work is 'supposed' to be blind to many differences of race, gender, religion and culture, but often is not. In one team, it may really not be an issue that one of the six is a woman. In another team, this may cause problems as the woman is partially excluded; perhaps she goes home to her children while the men go to the pub, they use sporting metaphors that she finds irritating.

A dysfunctional team will tend to be weak on most or all of the qualities listed above and will probably communicate poorly. A fully functional team will be strong on all the above components and communicate effectively. There is probably a synergy about team building, so that as a team improves in some areas of functioning, it will tend to improve also in other areas. For example, having clear goals is likely to improve team purpose. In a dysfunctional team, weaknesses in some areas will tend to weaken other areas. For example, poor interpersonal relationships will tend to weaken team commitment.

It is also important that the personal needs of individual team members are met in a team, as far as this is appropriate in the work environment. Another key issue is that the team resolves issues about inequalities of the status of team members within the organisation. Team members will vary in seniority, in power, in knowledge and experience, and in relevant communication skills. Staff with more of these qualities may be inclined to dominate group meetings and staff with less of these qualities may be inclined to defer to them. It is important that the team tries to develop so that everybody feels free to communicate, to disagree with others and to have their perspective acknowledged and considered. The ideal is that this occurs without repercussions, but this may be difficult to live up to in reality.

Most teams probably have some strengths and some weaknesses. For example, a team may have commitment and good problem-solving and decision-making skills but lack smooth interpersonal relationships and openness. They will probably work effectively on existing work tasks, but have difficulties if change is required. Another team may get along extremely well, but be weak on problem-solving and have unclear goals. Although the team will provide useful social support for its members, it may not accomplish much or reach decisions easily.

Dysfunctional teams

Here are sketches of some dysfunctional teams that you will no doubt recognise, as most of us have been members of such teams at some time.

Pre-teams

Members of the team communicate and relay information to each other with decision-making procedures followed through. The team, however, lacks a sense of purpose and the concept of shared learning is deficient. One might say that the team simply muddles along, doing its work as it always has. This could be called the 'pre-team' and represents the norm in many workplaces. Better teamworking may however be required in today's complex, global and rapidly changing society.

Pseudo-teams

A more extreme dysfunctional team is where members have no interest in developing a purpose to meet, and task objectives are clearly deficient. The members are uninterested in the concept of team building, which they see as extra work and disruptive. Marie remembers being involved in attempts to change organisational culture when she was brought in by senior management to set up and lead a research team in a research inactive department. Unfortunately, the members of the team lacked relevant experience and felt insecure and hostile about that, but were unwilling to discuss their anxieties openly. Her research skills were perceived as a threat and challenge to the other team members, rather than as complementary to their skills. The department had a history of conflict over excessive teaching loads and tended to be authoritarian in management style. For these reasons, there was a serious lack of interest and motivation in even agreeing team goals, which made the task of achieving anything very difficult. Katzenbach and Smith (1993) refers to this type of dysfunctional team as the 'pseudo-team'.

Potential teams

A third type of dysfunctional team is one where the members would like to perform well as a team but lack defined goals and direction. Katzenbach and Smith (1993) refers to this as the 'potential team'. One might say that the potential team never gets beyond scene-setting. For example, Richard was involved in a working group to develop a module for a new medical curriculum, which was going to use problem-based learning – where students decide what to find out to understand problems they are set – and teach all subjects together. All the people involved were keen to do this but it took about six months to learn how to develop problem-based learning goals across different disciplines. Initially, each person brought incompatible goals from their own discipline and regular and repetitive conflict ensued.

Getting teams to work

How does a dysfunctional team move to become a functional team? This is no easy task as the group is already formed and there are established roles. The best approach appears to be to work on communication skills first, assuming that only if the team communicates effectively is it possible to develop effective goals, purpose and working practices.

The first stage in developing a more effective team is to examine the interpersonal skills of the team and the existing group dynamics with a view to improving them. According to Woodcock (1979) at the early stages of team development the team will often show a number of fundamental weaknesses, including poor listening skills, unclear objectives and dependence on the leader to make most of the decisions. These weaknesses clearly have to reduce if an effective team is to emerge.

The second stage then should focus on building up good interpersonal skills whereby members are encouraged to show concern and interest for each other, better listening skills, self-disclosure and openness. Hopefully, this allows scene-setting discussions to occur and difficulties to be raised and dealt with.

At stage three, scene-setting and more methodical work procedures are implemented according to a clear and agreed set of ground rules. This will include the open discussion of problems and difficulties. It is worth noting that 'open' means that team members should feel free to raise whatever problems they are concerned about.

Finally, at stage four, the team begins to function properly. Once again, easier said than done!

It is probably easier to build an effective team from scratch than to turn an existing group of colleagues into an effective team. An existing group will have long-standing problems, routines and practices that may make team building difficult or impossible. For example interpersonal problems may be well entrenched and the people involved may have long-standing methods of dealing – dysfunctionally – with each other.

Structurally dysfunctional groups

So far, we have looked at how group communication occurs and the difficulties involved in it. We will now look at some of the ways that groups can go wrong which involve factors other than poor communication, or lack of team building. Groups can be dysfunctional because they are pre-teams, pseudo-teams or potential teams, but they can also be dysfunctional for more structural reasons to do with how they fit into the organisation.

In the workplace, it is often more appropriate to disband a dysfunctional group than to try and change it, but this may not be feasible, as staff cannot always be moved. We will offer some simple suggestions about how to change dysfunctional groups.

Often, when groups do not function well individual group members are blamed. Whilst difficult, unco-operative people certainly exist, research on why people behave in difficult or unco-operative ways tends to find that this is usually a product of the social situation, rather than the individual's personality. If group members misbehave, then this is often a sign of communication difficulties, as discussed earlier in the book, or other difficulties, outlined here. It is common for different members of a group to blame each other for difficulties. The manager may feel that the staff are difficult and the staff may feel that the manager is incompetent. Before engaging in such blaming, which can worsen the problem, it may be useful to ask if the group is a functional one. If it is structurally dysfunctional, then there are likely to be problems, no matter how skilled everybody is at communicating with each other and how well they get along on the personal level.

We suggest that there are four types of structurally dysfunctional group. Each will be described briefly, some suggestions for identifying them will be made and the basic ways of repairing them will be given. They are:

- Functionless groups
- Powerless groups
- Cults and cliques
- Dictatorships.

Functionless groups

Some groups do not accomplish anything because they do not have any clear goals or purpose. While social groups can have relatively vague goals, groups and meetings at work are supposed to occur for some sort of reason. If nobody is clear what this is then there will be problems.

General departmental or staff meetings can sometimes be like this; all the decisions are made elsewhere, staff are kept informed by memos and e-mails and the meeting is supposed to be run as a formal forum that discourages the discussion of new ideas. However, because this cannot be made clear to staff – the fiction of staff involvement would be exposed – some staff will try to express their viewpoints during the meeting. Such viewpoints will not be acknowledged properly (decisions having been made elsewhere) which encourages contributions of excessive length, as people seek acknowledgement of their ideas and feelings that is not forthcoming. Furthermore in the absence of group decision-making goals, staff will tend to work to personal goals that seem of marginal relevance to others.

Signs that a group lacks clear functions include:

- Some members make rather irrelevant contributions of excessive length.

- Some members raise essentially the same points at every meeting.
- When discussion occurs, it tends to focus on abstract and ideological issues, rather than concrete and practical ones, or specific issues of how people are feeling.
- Other members make no contribution at all, or regularly fail to attend, and this includes some senior members.
- Decisions are never made; at best, points are accepted for further consideration.
- Decisions made elsewhere regularly render group discussions irrelevant.
- People's feelings are not adequately acknowledged or dealt with.

The basic solution is to determine the group's purpose, which may be different from that which was supposed. If the departmental meeting's real purpose is to get feedback from staff about decisions made elsewhere – feedback that may or may not have an effect – then the meeting should be organised and structured accordingly. If the meeting's purpose is to allow staff to vent their grievances, then this too should be clear. If an informal interest group that meets at the end of the working day to discuss specialist issues evolves into being a social group that goes to the pub, then this too may be valid, but it is a waste of time to pretend to discuss the specialist issues first.

Powerless groups

Some groups run effectively and have clear goals, but have not been provided with the power to enact their decisions. As we saw in Chapter 8, power can be based on physical force, economic force, control of information, or authority. Let us take, for example, a working group to develop a workplace policy on sexual harassment. If the group consists of relatively junior staff, then they may be unable to persuade the organisation to follow their recommendations, or the organisation may accept the recommendations on paper but provide no sanctions if they are violated. The working group may recommend the appointment of a sexual harassment officer, but no funds for this post are forthcoming. The group may require that all departments make regular returns about sexual harassment, but returns are either not supplied, or consistently deny any such occurrences. The sexual harassment officer appointed may be a senior male manager, who has been 'promoted sideways' because he was a liability in his previous post. As he is not taken seriously as a manager, or as a useful spokesperson for harassment, women never approach him for advice on these issues. Nonetheless he chairs the working group, discrediting it.

Signs that a group lacks power include:

- There are no channels by which it can negotiate or communicate with the rest of the organisation.
- Somebody else, or another group in the organisation, takes reports from the group, but there is no obvious outcome, or feedback.
- The group has no control over financial resources.
- It lacks any special expertise; indeed group members may be unclear as to why they in particular were required to work in the group.
- It does not include any staff more senior than the staff who will have to enact its decisions (assuming that the organisation does not use a radically flat structure).
- The group is not consulted about its interests before decisions are made elsewhere in the organisation.

The basic solution here is to create power for the group, which involves developing some or all of the preceding resources. Work can be done to develop channels of communication, reports need to be followed up and feedback requested. The group should attempt to obtain and get control over a budget. The group should develop expertise and try to involve senior staff. When the group is not consulted then it should politely object and point out the benefits to the organisation that would have occurred if they had been consulted.

Creating power should not be confused with seizing power. The former assumes that others in the organisation will continue to have power and that this is appropriate. Seizing power is the attempt to maximise the power of the group and minimise the power of others. The group will impose its view, to the best of its ability. It will attempt to channel and control information originating elsewhere. Financial control over others will be taken by getting as much of the resources available as possible (not just whatever is necessary) and by attempting to control the groups where other groups' resources are decided. Efforts will be taken to display the power and expertise of the group, while also discrediting the power and expertise of others. The group will not only demand that it is consulted, but may attempt to turn all decisions to its own interests. When all groups have adequate power, then this will probably benefit most organisations. Seizure of power will generally benefit the powerful group more than the organisation, and may result in many of the problems discussed in Chapter 8.

Cults and cliques

Some groups are dysfunctional because they operate as a cult or a clique. This often happens in a group that has seized power, but it can also happen elsewhere. A cult or clique has two basic characteristics. First, that it is a cohesive group where group loyalties are paramount and dissent is not tolerated. This makes 'groupthink' (see Chapter 9) likely. Second, that the group has beliefs that differ from those held by the rest of the world. Well-known cults tend to have beliefs that seem strange and unrealistic to the rest of the world, such as that the world will end on a particular date. However, many cliques in the workplace are formed around exaggerated, but not particularly strange, beliefs such as the importance of the specific work that the clique does, or the wonderfulness of the group's leader.

The main characteristics of a clique are:

- Strong emphasis on social cohesion, to the extent that factual disagreements are seen as disloyal to the group.
- Sanctions imposed against people who disagree with the group.
- Strong perceptions of superiority, of some kind, over the out-group.
- Group beliefs that do not fit in with the views of the rest of the organisation, and are resistant to change.

Junior staff working in the same office or factory floor sometimes form a clique based on assumptions like the following:

- We need to stick together or the management will get us.
- Other people are out to exploit us.
- We do all the essential work around here.
- Our current work practices suit us better than any alternatives.
- We know more about our work than anybody else.

One example of this is the 'Bank Wiring Group' of workers who developed clear norms about work output rates. Workers who deviated from the norms were sanctioned, as were inspectors and supervisors (see McKenna, 1998: 317–18). Even if a clique has a reasonably rational view of the world, it is likely to be unco-operative when change is necessary, even if the change will benefit the clique. It may also take a highly negative view of people outside the clique, which can create difficulties when interactions with them are required. For example, the advice of experts from outside the clique may be discredited or ignored, unless it fits with existing group thinking.

Sometimes workplace teams develop exaggerated views of their leader and the specific project that they are engaged in. This form of distortion can be worsened by only hiring people who are very positive about the project, and discouraging dissent to the point that more critical staff tend to leave. Common unifying beliefs for this type of clique include:

- Our leader is a genius.
- The work that we do, or the project that we are engaged in, is uniquely important.
- The fact that our work has yet to bear fruit is due to external difficulties, such as lack of funds or appreciation.
- Our work is absolutely central to our organisation, but this is not as yet appreciated.

We have seen examples of such beliefs being maintained in the face of very clear counter-evidence; the leader frequently makes obvious blunders, nobody else thinks that the work is important and the work of the team comprises a fraction of a percentage of the expenditure of the organisation. The team that change the world after a long struggle and general contempt for them is a romantic story, often-told in Hollywood, but the realities of success are usually more mundane. Most successful work in science as much as business involves hard work along the same lines as your rivals.

Rather as personality disorders are resistant to change, so too are cults or cliques. The basic way of changing them is to open them up to the outside world, but such groups are likely to resist this. Methods that can be tried include bringing in new members with different ideas, changing leadership and retraining clique members, but members may try and convert others instead. If it is not possible to disband the clique, then sometimes it may be necessary to simply leave them alone and work around them. Besides, what if they turned out to be correct all along?

Dictatorships

Many workplace groups are headed by a strong manager whose role is to direct the work of staff, to appraise that work and to make decisions. Such autocratic management can be appropriate, and many organisations deliberately structure themselves in this way.

However, it can be seen as problematic when workplace groups that are supposed to operate collectively are run autocratically in practice, usually, but not always, with the manager as dictator. The signs of a dictatorship are too obvious to elaborate: the boss imposes his or her will on other team members.

One can either accept the dictator as benign, or restructure the group to remove the dictator and rebuild the team. To accept a dictator as benign, one needs to establish that the group actually is working well as a dictatorship. Are the other group members happy with the situation? Is work done well and effectively? Is the group sufficiently flexible? Can the dictator cope sufficiently with the role? Or is he or she on the way to becoming a workaholic, or unable to delegate anything, or making excessive demands on other staff? Could the organisation cope if the dictator left? We suspect that at least some of these questions will usually be answered 'no', but occasionally an individual may be so exceptional and talented that it is appropriate to allow them to run a group their way.

Disadvantages of teamworking

Teamworking – that is smooth group working – is both a good and a necessary thing from the perspective of any organisation that wants work to occur effectively. However, from the perspective of the employee teamworking can have some disadvantages. Working in a team of people who communicate effectively with each other sounds nice, maybe preferable to what occurs at your work, but it:

• Is a high standard to live up to.
• Can be even more stressful when things go wrong.
• Can be over-demanding of staff time and effort.
• Includes a strong component of 'emotional labour' that can make jobs more demanding and exploitative.

The strain of high standards

Famously, Christmas is a stressful time in many families as the gap between the fantasy happy family and your squabbling brood becomes more apparent than ever. Being expected to be a team can place similar strain on a workplace that previously muddled through and got the job done despite dysfunctional communication and all sorts of interpersonal feuds, rather like *Drop the Dead Donkey*. The idea of a team makes this look inadequate to 'team members' and, more worryingly may bring criticism from senior management, who previously left well enough alone as long as the job got done. Dilbert

(Adams, 1997) names 'teamwork' as one of the 'harbingers of doom' for your company.

Stress when things go wrong

If you expect your colleagues to be selfish and nasty, then at least you will not be disappointed. When things go wrong in a team, then this may involve people whom you have come to care about and expect a lot of. Naturally, this makes problems more stressful. For example, when two of your colleagues run off taking several prize accounts with them, and it turns out that they have been conducting a clandestine affair, then this can generate a bit of excitement for most staff. In contrast, their team may be shattered by the betrayal. Even more mundane things, like moving job, can become difficult.

Demands on time and effort

Teamwork may require socialising after work, effort to support others on the team and many other demands that make it difficult for somebody to 'do their job and draw their pay' without excessive commitment. Management teams may be paid so well that the organisation's expectations about commitment seem fair enough, but many other teams may be expected to make substantial additional commitment without additional compensation. Does the food services team really want to spend their whole weekend on team building exercises, when they have spent eight hours a day in the fast-food restaurant?

Emotional labour

This is a relatively new idea. An increasing number of jobs demand that staff make an emotional commitment to the work, as well as commitment of time and effort. The two most common kinds of emotional labour are the requirement to enjoy and be positive about your work and the expectation that you should deal effectively and pleasantly with customers' problems. Teamwork is particularly likely to lead to expectations about enjoying work. These may be appropriate when the work is genuinely challenging and well paid, but may simply be extra demands when it is not. Indeed many highly demanding workplaces, including the police, the health services and the social services thrive on black humour, cynicism about clients and a careful distancing of the self from the work. Total emotional commitment to such work might be excessive and ultimately counter-productive.

In short, teamwork can require staff to commit too much of themselves to their work. At worst, teamworking can be used as a device to get more work out of people, rather than a means of improving the quality of work and the working environment.

Conclusions

All well-functioning workplace groups will resemble teams, suggesting that teams are necessary for much work. Developing a fully functioning team is difficult and requires considerable thought and effort. It is useful if a team contains a complementary mixture of skills, knowledge and personalities and effective, open communication within a team must be developed. However, none of this guarantees a fully functioning team. There are also some costs to teamwork, mainly to do with the higher demands that it can place upon staff.

Exercises

Effective team building

What is effective team building? List a minimum of five techniques essential for effective team building and try to provide a brief description of why they are important. Compare your list with those of colleagues or friends.

Hiring staff that complement your team

Taking a workplace group or team from your own experience, what type of person would you ideally hire to complement the existing skills and personalities? Why?

Dysfunctional teams or groups

Drawing on your own experience, think of an example of a work team or group that functioned very poorly. Using hindsight and the information in this chapter, draw up a list of the factors that you think contributed to the group's poor functioning. Remember that if you find yourself blaming individuals, you may have failed to identify communication or structural problems.

Recommended reading

Belbin, R.M. (1981) *Management Teams – Why They Succeed or Fail*, Oxford: Heinemann.

Katzenbach, J.R. and Smith, D.K. (1993) *The Wisdom of Teams*, Cambridge, MA: Harvard Business School.

McKenna, E. (1998) *Business Psychology and Organisational Behaviour*, Hove, East Sussex: Psychology Press.

Woodcock, M. (1979) *Team Development Manual*, London: Gower.

12 Group communications in networked society

In this chapter we will look at how work has changed recently, how electronic communications are evolving and what implications these have for group communication at work.

Objectives

By the end of the chapter you should:

- Know the basic ways that work has changed in networked society.
- Understand how communication functions in cyberspace.
- Appreciate the limits of electronic communications.

Work in network society

There have been massive changes in the use of computer technology at work and the economy over the past thirty years, which have transformed the nature of work and the nature of most organisations (Castells, 1998). The most relevant changes for this book include:

- The globalisation of organisations and their markets.
- Widespread use of rapid, remote communications including telephone sales, faxes, mobile phones, e-mail and the internet.
- Widespread automation of aspects of communication, including automatic stock control and ordering, computer-assisted telephone helplines and answering services, automated customer processing via the internet, computerised invoicing and sales systems, as well as automatic financial transfers and record keeping.

These changes have in turn changed the nature of the social interactions that occur in the workplace.

More interactions tend to be with people who are based far away

You may never even meet some of them, or have hardly met them. These can include important people, such as senior managers and technicians who provide you with support. They may come from markedly different cultures to you. Although these remote interactions can be important and influential, they will tend to lack the interpersonal richness of face-to-face communication and will only rarely involve group interactions, as video conferencing is still too expensive to be routine except for very senior managers in affluent organisations.

The medium of communication is less often face to face

It is more often over the telephone or in writing (via fax, letter, e-mail or computer form). We will look at communication in cyberspace and the nature of groups there later on in this chapter. Culture in cyberspace is still evolving and it is still unclear whether groups in cyberspace meet the social functions of face-to-face groups.

Some of the work duties that used to involve face-to-face interaction, now only require minimal interactions, or have been replaced by human–computer interactions

This tends to make routine workplace communications quicker and easier, but may reduce the formation of interpersonal relationships, reduce the opportunities for normal social interaction at work (which increase job satisfaction), reduce the formation of cohesive workplace groups and make dealing with unusual events or problems slower and more difficult.

In short, communications nowadays are more likely to be remote and to not involve substantial interpersonal contact or face-to-face group discussion. They are also more likely to be routine or automated in character. Referring back to Chapter 8, studies of obedience and social roles imply that *remote, automated* communications are likely to diminish the sense that one is interacting with another person of equal value. This in turn may lead to some of the more unfortunate aspects of interpersonal behaviour including self-seeking behaviour, minimising the other person's point of view, excessive obedience to authority and a diminished sense of individual responsibility for one's actions. At minimum, this is liable to lead to communications that leave at least one party dissatisfied.

One example we have noticed of such trends is in our interactions with financial institutions in recent years. Over this period many institutions have centralised many of their procedures, meaning that local branches, even where they exist, mainly refer decisions and other work to the centre. Branches of banks, building societies and insurers appear to be set up to deal efficiently with the provision of routine services to customers, using standard forms and automated procedures. If things go wrong, or there is anything required that is out of the routine, then repeated phone calls may be required to find somebody who is willing and able to deal with it. Unfortunately, while staff are usually polite, their response to non-routine enquiries is to pass them on to someone else, who often then fails to reply, or passes the problem on again. Sometimes nobody seems willing or able to take personal responsibility for the customer's case, and concern about delays, errors and inefficiencies often seems minimal.

In the context of routine, automated communications, groups and teams in an organisation will continue to serve important social functions, along with their specific roles, duties and responsibilities. Social functions will include creating a sense of group cohesion, identity and purpose, as well as meeting individuals' needs for normal social support and interaction. It is not currently possible to anticipate when and if such functions will be taken over by alternative forms of communication. As we will see shortly, despite the fascination of e-mail and discussion lists, these are not yet fully serving group functions.

Communication in cyberspace

Until recently, communicating with more than one other person at a time could only happen face to face, or so slowly (by circulating documents for example) that dynamic interaction was limited. Information technology has now introduced a number of methods for electronic group communications that are revolutionising the ways that people interact. In a networked society, interaction, identity, communicative roles and channels of communication all change. The internet will continue to affect the ways that we work and interact. We will write of 'cyberspace' as the general label for all the new electronic means of communicating, to convey the sense that cyberspace has extension, like real space, but that as far as communication is concerned the rules of time and space are different there.

According to Castells (1996: ch. 5) the number of people who interact in cyberspace is growing. However, it is difficult to estimate how many regular users there are, as opposed to people who have access to the technology but do not use it, or who make very occasional and limited use of it. At this time, most users have been introduced to cyberspace for reasons connected with their work, although the rise of web access for the cost of a local call may change that. It is likely that things will evolve so that there will be a small elite skilled workforce who interact in cyberspace, and a much larger proportion of society who will mainly be passive consumers of cyberculture, for example via digital TV. One can guess that the ability to use cyberspace effectively will become paramount in many workplaces.

There is enormous interest in electronic communication, it is developing very rapidly and research can barely keep up with the changes. This section sketches an overview of the nature of group communication in cyberspace that allows you to understand the fundamental differences between face-to-face and electronic communication.

A case history

Universities were among the first institutions to have e-mail facilities and probably still make more use of cyberspace than many other organisations. By now both of us use e-mail more than either printed letters or memos, or telephone calls.

We will use Richard as a case history. On an average day he receives about three pieces of real mail (not circulars or advertising) and sends only one or two; he makes or receives about 5 phone calls. He receives about 15 e-mails, of which about 10 are not circulars or advertising, and sends about five replies. He also receives one or two e-mails from mailing lists that he subscribes to, but does not necessarily read them, or reply to them at the time. Occasionally, he reads correspondence from a number of discussion lists on topics that interest him, but doesn't usually reply or get involved. Another important use of e-mail is that many messages he sends and receives now have 'attachments', which contain documents of various kinds. He often reads or edits them and sends them back. Over the past year he has worked on many projects this way, both with people who work in the same building and with people who work all over Britain and even all over the world. Gradually in the past few years, writing joint articles has involved less time spent meeting to discuss the writing and more time spent communicating electronically. It can even be convenient to communicate this way with the person in the next office, or with your spouse, if you are writing a book together!

He also uses an internet browser about three or four times a day, usually to look things up, but occasionally to order things such as books or computer software. Most of this use involves little interaction with other people. He is also involved in developing a website for distance learning, so he spends some hours a week looking at that. He also wastes at least an hour a week, although usually only minutes at a time, cursing software that has crashed or failed to do what he wanted. But these are not yet communicative activities.

Like many people, Richard is spending more time on remote communicative activities rather than face-to-face communications. Why? The following are what he sees as the advantages and disadvantages of cyberspace communications.

Advantages of cyberspace communications

- Saves time spent trying to contact people – they can answer e-mail when they are free, rather than having to keep seeking a reply.
- Saves time spent dealing with routine enquiries – e-mail can be dealt with when convenient.
- Cheap for contacts with people who work far away.
- Convenient for contacts with people who live in different time zones, who can reply when they are at work.
- Can be less stressful than face-to-face interaction, particularly for people who have low status at work, or lack confidence.
- Allows a considered response that may be better than a spontaneous response in a face-to-face interaction.
- Convenient for sending draft material for others to revise.
- A lot of up-to-date specialist information sources can be accessed and browsed online that would be difficult to obtain from libraries.
- You can read about and look at pictures of things before buying them.
- The stock of many on-line companies is better than their physical counterparts.

Disadvantages of cyberspace communications

- Time wasted tinkering with the computer – for example trying to open attachments – rather than on real work.
- Time wasted browsing irrelevant but interesting material.
- Costs in time, money and knowledge of maintaining a modern web-compatible computer.
- Lack of immediate feedback can make communication difficult.
- It is more difficult to assess the sincerity or nature of correspondents whom you do not already know.
- Time wasted circulating too many drafts of things, because it is easier to do so than finish them.

- The reliability of information on the web can be difficult to assess and many sites do not work properly – for example, the links given are out of date.
- Takes up time that could be spent on face-to-face interactions and diminishes local contacts (although e-mail may supplement rather than replace face-to-face meetings; Brotherton, 1999: 157).

For Richard, the advantages clearly outweigh the disadvantages, but he likes using computers and enjoys putting in the time and effort to learn how to use them properly. This is not true of everyone who makes use of the internet.

Communicative roles in cyberspace

There is no longer simply a 'speaker' and one or more 'listeners'. The 'speaker' may indeed speak, but is more likely to type information on a computer keyboard, or transmit documents written or copied earlier. It is more sensible to refer to the *originator* of the message. There are also a number of *receivers* of the message. Discussion lists consist of originators who send messages, active receivers who receive and reply to messages and *lurkers* who receive messages but do not reply to them.

Lurking, or eavesdropping, is somewhat impolite and socially unskilled in face-to-face communication but is the social norm in cyberspace. Most people in cyberspace spend most of their time lurking, connecting to websites, but not signing the guestbook; looking at discussion lists, but deciding not to participate; trashing e-mail without replying to it and so on. Lurking is the norm because otherwise you would be overwhelmed with information.

Also, unlike face-to-face interactions, many communications in cyberspace begin with a message from an originator that is the equivalent of standing shouting in a bar and hoping that other people strike up a conversation. Outside cyberspace it is antisocial, even a sign of madness, to frequently transmit messages without having a chosen receiver. Somebody who does this in the street is suspected of being drunk or schizophrenic. In cyberspace this is a normal way of starting up an interaction: most personal websites, and many commercially successful ones, began with someone setting out some information and hoping that people would find the site interesting or entertaining. Messages to lists often start 'Does anyone . . .?'

Cyberspace is often portrayed as the endless hum of information being exchanged. While loads of information are indeed exchanged, it is against the background of, at any given moment, many more people lurking and others originating information without knowing if anyone wants to read it. Every so often people connect with each other.

Groups in cyberspace

Because of this strange nature of communication in cyberspace, social groups and meetings are very different there. First, group membership is often uncertain, because one cannot be sure who is lurking, or who is about to contribute. Nor can one be certain about the authorship of material on many sites. Second, meetings are often *asynchronous*, that is they occur without members being fully-synchronised in the time course of the interaction. Third, meetings have unclear boundaries in time. Many originators try to initiate interactions, but most fail to develop beyond trivial exchanges. Even after a discussion has seemingly 'ended' other people may make contributions, sometimes days later.

The concept of a *thread* is important here. A thread, or threaded discussion, is the normal means by which a group of people interact in cyberspace. Here, someone originates a message, which is replied to by a number of other people, and in turn replied to again, like a face-to-face conversation. Sometimes, all this happens smoothly and rapidly, like most face-to-face interaction. Sometimes it happens very asynchronously, because all cyber communications tend to be recorded and stored. For example, someone can send a question to a discussion list. Months later, someone else may read the question and send an answer. The answer may trigger a reply from the originator, that in turn causes a brief discussion involving several people. This then quietens down. A few weeks later, someone else reads the first message and sends a new reply. There is then another flurry of activity, but this time it consists of other people reprimanding the new originator for not bothering to read the later discussion before originating a message. This sort of asynchronous activity can occur even when the original discussion was supposed to occur all of an afternoon, as long as it was stored and the new originator was in a position to read it. And, from the point of view of a new reader, the discussion thread, originally spread over months, can all seem to occur within a few minutes.

Threaded discussions among a limited number of people, all of whom read and contribute to the discussion, can come to resemble real-time cooperative learning and be used, for example, instead of seminars (English and Yazdani, 1999). The principles for effective group work discussed in earlier chapters still apply here. The group needs a sense of cohesion and agreed goals, among other things, and training is probably necessary (Susman, 1998). Because of the possibility of lurking, it is also necessary to point out what would be self-evident in face-to-face groups: you cannot expect to have a cohesive group discussion on an open e-mail list where you are interrupted by children and passers-by. Nor can you run a coherent electronic discussion group if group members do not contribute regularly. Many electronic 'discussion groups' barely rise to the level of conversation. Instead, they are limited to different people making announcements, or asking questions, perhaps getting a reply and then 'discussion' moves on to something else. Asking the world your questions is quite useful, but it is not 'discussion'.

Asynchronous threaded discussion has however created a novel way of communicating that lies halfway between the considered letter and the spontaneous telephone conversation. Maybe it has merely rediscovered the art of letter writing as practised in the nineteenth century before the telegraph was invented, but when there were several postal deliveries a day and people could communicate by letter across London and receive a reply later in the day.

Synchronous groups in cyberspace

Synchronous groups are situations where communication between people occurs in real time. They are technically much more complex to manage than asynchronous groups because of *bandwidth* problems, which are difficulties in managing the large quantity of information required to communicate in real time. It is sometimes suggested that as computer memories and processors get larger and faster, bandwidth problems will disappear. This will indeed allow the storage and transmission of more information faster, but that is not the only bandwidth problem. There are also problems of recording synchronous communication between several people. Simply pointing a microphone, or video camera, at each of them is not always enough because electronic recording devices cannot as yet intelligently compensate for deficiencies in the speaker's transmission. When speakers look away, put their hands over their mouths, speak all at the same time, or mumble we still understand, but what is recorded can be unintelligible. The other bandwidth problem that is difficult to solve is the problem of displaying synchronous communication in some reasonably compact format. The current 'ideal' might be to have a screen to display each speaker but this is unlikely for most computer users and impracticable in situations where one does not know how many people will be participating. Putting up windows on a normal computer screen can rapidly lead to windows that are too small to see everybody clearly. Using audio only, or typing creates similar problems that we will not detail. Bandwidth problems mean that it will be some time before synchronous communication can provide the richness that we take for granted face to face. Meantime, its somewhat crude nature will tend to restrict the extent to which it is used.

There are basically two types of synchronous group in current use, video conferencing and virtual chat rooms.

VIDEO CONFERENCING

Video conferencing involves the use of computers to establish a visual link between two or more locations, which allows people to see and hear each other for interaction. There are currently two technical and financial limitations on video conferencing. First, for the interaction to resemble a face-to-face group, it is necessary to have camera operators who can track who is speaking, or enough cameras to fix one on each participant. This is too expensive (hundreds or thousands of pounds per hour) to be a routine option in most organisations. Second, as the video information is transmitted down a telephone it is digitised and sampled. This gives a somewhat jerky and unnatural feel to the video, which many readers will have seen in video samples on computers. Richard has recently experimented with the use of a simple video link for teaching and the following is a brief account of that experience.

Teaching a course remotely using an ISDN video link   Rather than using multiple cameras and operators, the TV service at the University of Sheffield provided a simple set-up that I could operate almost unaided; just a fixed camera, a computer and a video monitor. Therefore course delivery was inexpensive in terms of technical support and teaching was largely unimpeded by technical problems – I have had more difficulties using a video recorder and slide projector. Costs were restricted to the costs of the telephone call and rental fees for the equipment and studio. For the teacher, a modicum of computer literacy is essential and some previous TV experience would be helpful. The course involved six two-hour sessions over six weeks.

Because the video is sampled the picture is rather jerky and of relatively low quality, but by the second session both the students and I were used to this. The students, based at the University of Wales,

Swansea, sat in a room and viewed me projected slightly larger than life, if of lower quality, on the wall. They found it harder to engage with me than they would have face to face and it was helpful that the course organiser sat in on most of the sessions. At first he had to occasionally push students to contribute to discussion. By about week four things felt much more natural for them. The only other problem at the student end was that the bright lighting required to video them meant that their room became very hot. In Sheffield, I was in the TV service's large and comfortable studio so this was not a problem, although it was warm enough that I needed a good supply of water. Some other problems and how we overcame them are worth describing.

Starting with the obvious, you need someone else to focus the camera on you before the session begins and ensure that you are properly in shot. This only takes a minute. The video link is prone to crash. This usually happens when the phone connection is being established. I had to restart the computer, then the connection would always establish all right. Occasionally, the link crashed in the middle of a class – three times in the six weeks. Restarting the computer and reconnecting sorted this out within two or three minutes. This was only mildly irritating and there are often technical glitches during teaching, so this is no barrier to using the system.

I viewed the students on a large TV monitor, with myself displayed on a mercifully small screen-within-screen box. Keeping things simple, we used a fixed camera at both ends. There were seven students on the course so they were all viewable at once, but you could only manage up to about ten students on camera with their faces large enough to make out. Even with seven, it was sometimes difficult to see who was speaking, so we got them to put up their hands when making a contribution. I think that with larger groups at least one camera operator would be required at the student end. A related problem is that as faces appear smaller in video, you lose the more subtle aspects of facial expression. The screen-within-screen shows a mirror image. Eventually I worked out why – when I looked at a student then my screen mirror projection also looked the same way. A non-mirrored image would have looked the wrong way and that would have disrupted natural communication. I had to work a little at not monitoring my image too much.

The mirror image was a bit problematic because we were using a visualiser – a video camera on a stand that can serve as an overhead projector, or display objects – to show 'overheads' and other material. I couldn't read my overheads projected backwards, quite small on the screen so I had to look sideways at the originals. Not really a major problem. I recommend the use of a visualiser because I think it would be monotonous to look at a 'talking head' for two hours. I could switch between the camera on me and the visualiser, so students saw one or the other. We didn't use video tapes or anything like that, but this would be easy to set up by switching to another video source.

By about week four, we were interacting quite naturally despite the somewhat inhibiting technical set-up. For teaching style I found it tricky that I had to sit in a relatively fixed position, while at the same time rather over-acting and over-emoting to compensate for the slightly impoverished communicative medium. It was quite tiring, compared to an equivalent face-to-face session. With further practice it would become more routine. Gestures require particular thought. Waving my hands about as normal looked stupid on sampled video, but not using gestures at all looked boring.

Overall, the special technical problems were relatively minor and with a little practice teaching became quite transparent. If the class were slightly harder to warm up than normal, then they were no harder to warm up than many face-to-face classes that I have taught. Students were generally positive about the course. Although we were apprehensive, the use of the ISDN link was far from being the best of a bad job, rather it is a good way of remote teaching, particularly for smaller groups where two-way interaction is required.

The general messages of this experience are that video can be used for effective group interactions, as long as the group is not too large. The information available for communication is reduced, but sufficient information is left for communications to occur quite naturally after a little practice. It is probably necessary to compensate somewhat by changing communicative style, particularly its non-verbal components, and by signalling clearly who is speaking and whose turn it is to speak (see Preece *et al.*, 1994: ch. 9 for further discussion). Other than that the principles of group communication discussed throughout this book probably apply adequately to video links.

VIRTUAL CHAT ROOMS

Another type of group is the virtual chat room. This is software that allows a number of people to chat – type short messages – to each other in near real time. The internet contains a growing number of chat rooms of various kinds. At bare minimum, virtual chat can simply be an agreement among a group of people to all be connected at the same time and send e-mails to each other very rapidly. This can happen in close to real time, but not closely enough for turn-taking to occur smoothly. There are also much more sophisticated environments for chat. For example 'The Palace' (see Suler, 1999) is a software system that allows users to move about a virtual environment that contains different rooms and spaces, chatting to the other people they find there. People appear in The Palace as cartoon representations called 'avitars', some of which can be complex and produce visual signals to augment typed communication. These signals may eventually make up for the lack of verbal and non-verbal cues on the internet, but they remain relatively unsophisticated and an agreed code of signification is only just developing among users.

The use of avitars is a particularly obvious manifestation of the trend on the internet for people to adopt social roles that differ markedly from those that they use face to face. For example, people may pretend to be a different sex, particularly as the internet remains male dominated and women can find it more convenient to suggest that they are men, while men may get more attention by suggesting that they are women.

While interesting, the primary focus of The Palace is playful, indeed 'dreamlike' (Suler, 1999) and it as yet seems unsuited to use in the workplace. In our brief explorations of The Palace we could see the following problems:

Difficulties in turn-taking   As 'speech' arrives complete in a speech balloon, people cannot prepare to reply while somebody else is finishing speaking. Nor are there clear signals as to who is to speak next.

Banality   Many users of The Palace are passers-by, novices and (seemingly) children, who don't seem to have anything substantial to say. Many avitars lurk without saying anything. As in the corporeal world, to have a proper group discussion it would be necessary to agree to meet in a chat room and exclude passers-by.

Shyness   To new users the appearance of avitars is confusing, if interesting, and the social rules about them are unclear (although see Suler, 1999). This seems to inhibit communication, at least among newer users. We judge this on the basis that most visitors to The Palace don't seem to move far beyond the entrance, don't say much and don't stay long.

Self-referentiality   Much of the non-banal chat that occurs seems to be 'about' technical and social aspects of The Palace, such as how you design your avitar, which is the equivalent of meetings that mainly discuss how the meetings should be run.

There is clearly however the potential for such systems to evolve rules of communication that get around these difficulties and although chat rooms seem mainly of play and novelty value today, this may change very rapidly. It will be interesting to see what happens when teenagers who have grown up with virtual chat move into the world of work. They may find it natural to extend chat there. It would not be safe to speculate about how such real-time virtual groups will come to function.

The medium of communication in cyberspace

Because e-mail and other electronic communications can be exchanged very rapidly, almost in real time if you have a fast computer link, people can tend to forget that for their messages to be sent they have to be stored. In theory, everything that you communicate electronically is kept somewhere, at least for a while. Every receiver of your message also gets an exact copy of it that they can refer to later, or copy for their own purposes. People tend to be more spontaneous in e-mail than they would be in a printed letter. In face-to-face interactions spontaneous communications tend also to be ephemeral. Because they fade away, people tend to be less formal in how they express themselves and less cautious about what they say than they would be in a formal presentation. Literal transcripts of many committee meetings would make alarming reading! The committee secretary's duty is to convert spontaneous discourse into a formal, considered discussion.

Electronic communications can be spontaneous, but they may not be ephemeral. Records of e-mail discussions have been used in several recent court cases, including the Microsoft alleged monopoly case, to show managers discussing opponents in dangerously candid terms that they might not have committed directly to paper. It is worth remembering that what you write to somebody can be kept by them and, even if you trust them, sent to others, who in turn could send it on to yet others. E-mail can be transmitted like gossip, but as it stays literal it can be harder to deny. So, before you insult your boss to your best friend in another department, take a moment to worry about who else might read what you are sending. The potential also exists to monitor automatically all electronic communications (mobile phones too) for key words and record any communications where they come up. The technology exists for a suspicious company director to receive copies of all e-mails originating in the company that refer to him, although as far as we know such technology is as yet restricted to military and government security. Enough paranoia, but do consider that electronic communications may be permanently recorded.

The content of communication in cyberspace

The internet and e-mail have both evolved rapidly. As little as five years ago most of the internet appeared to be written by enthusiasts, who saw it as of intrinsic value. By now, commercial values are much more apparent. Some sites are directly commercial and offer wares for sale. Other sites use content of one kind or another to sell advertising space, rather as magazines do. So, much of the content of the internet is now advertising. However, there is also enormous diversity of content, covering every imaginable aspect of human interest including the major human staples such as sex, religion, food, drugs and money and innumerable minor eccentricities.[1] The most recent development is a rapid evolution of free internet connection providers, either funded by the costs of telephone line usage (e.g., Btnet), or by other commercial means – including advertising and direct sales facilities (e.g., Tesconet). We guess that websites that serve no commercial or other purpose for their authors will not survive long, but hope that we will continue to enjoy the many thousands of sites whose purposes are purely creative or communicative.

Commerce on many sites is possible entirely automatically, with no human communication at all. You order goods via an automatic form, using a credit card and receive an automatic e-mail acknowledgement. Presumably a person still puts your goods in a package, but if you've ordered software then you can download it yourself, register it, pay for it and have the payment deducted from your credit card without ever contacting a person. Many adverts on sites direct you to other sites where commerce is possible. For example, special interest sites are encouraged to link to Amazon or another online bookseller so that readers can easily order relevant books.

Such automatic or semi-automatic communications are bound to grow in sophistication and popularity. For example, at amazon.com, when you choose a book the site is structured to also suggest to you other books you might like, on the basis of what books other buyers have ordered together. Sites can automatically e-mail you when they change. Already sites can e-mail you and tell you that some product you might like is now available. The site for mp3 format compressed music files is one example: http://www.mp3.com. Such automated marketing techniques will become increasingly tailored to meet your individual wants and desires, as revealed by what you have ordered in the past and which web pages you have viewed; information that is routinely logged by most website management software. Such communication is one-sided. Computer software may be getting better at recording and guessing what the customer wants, but there is no give and take between the customer and the computer. Computers may already be better than many sales staff at looking up catalogues and guessing customer needs, but there is a risk that they eliminate the 'human touch'. Interpersonal communication is still required when the customer's needs are unclear or different from the assumptions written into the computer.

Features of interpersonal electronic communication

Electronic commerce may become increasingly automated, but meantime most traffic on the net is still interpersonal communication. According to Siegel *et al.* (1986) (quoted in Brotherton, 1999: 156–7) computer-mediated communication can lead to the following changes, which are all due to the relative absence of the social context information that is normally provided by verbal and non-verbal cues.

Uninhibited behaviour   This can include swearing and sexual references, as well as 'flaming', where somebody uses excessively strong language to disagree with someone else on a discussion list.

Depersonalisation (see de-individuation in Chapter 7)   This can lead to a failure to treat the other person as a human being with rights and needs equivalent to yours; failing to consider their point of view for example.

Reduced emotionality   Embarrassment, guilt and empathy may all be decreased. This may contribute to uninhibited behaviour of a kind that would be prevented by these feelings face to face. It can also enable discussion of topics that would be awkward face to face; e.g., there are discussion lists about sexual fetishes. Alternatively, some people fail to express positive emotions sufficiently in e-mail, producing messages that are excessively 'business like'.

Reduced comparisons with others and reduced fears of rejection   Writers can fail to monitor sufficiently the impression that they are creating. On the other hand, computer-mediated communications may suit people who tend to be fearful of rejection face to face.

This paints a rather negative picture of computer-mediated communication, so we should point out that the vast majority of e-mail communications are not like this. However, it is probably true that special effort is required to compensate for the lack of verbal and non-verbal cues. E-mail is still writing, and more like a letter than even a phone call, despite the speed with which e-mails can be exchanged. It is possible that these features of computer-mediated communication actually benefit people who may not perform well face to face because they are socially anxious, or treated as low status by their colleagues, or not verbally articulate. It can also be easier for people to disguise or downplay their status via e-mail and receive fairer treatment from others.

Netiquette

Many discussion lists provide some version of 'netiquette' that explains how to behave, and this is our version:

- Think about what you are saying.
- Include enough context for the receiver to know what you are referring to. 'Regarding your message: OK' may make no sense if the receiver sends and receives a lot of mail.
- Be appropriately brief and to the point.
- Be polite.
- Express emotion in a balanced way; neither failing to express any nor being over-emotional.
- Remember that people other than the intended receiver may see your message.
- It can help to make the effort to meet regular correspondents face to face, if this is possible.

Starting up communication in cyberspace

We also have some hints for starting up communications in cyberspace.

- Persist! If no one replies to your first communication then try again.
- Be cautious in what you disclose, remember it can easily be recorded and disseminated.
- Be patient. Communication is not as easy as face to face.
- When in doubt lurk. Lurking can allow you to discover how other people do it, and then you can try to imitate them.

- Return to threads of interest. Most threads will only interest you some of the time, other times they will be repetitive, banal, or involve discussion of the technical and communicative aspects of the thread.

Internet addiction

Finally, it is interesting that some people find the internet so reinforcing that they come to feel that they are 'addicted' to it. This phenomenon has now been fairly well documented (e.g., Griffiths, 1999). Internet addicts can spend large amounts of time on line, have enormous phone bills, think about being on line when they are not and neglect other activities to stay on line. Despite the limitations of electronic communication, it is clearly fascinating for many people in its diversity, complexity and in the possibility of communicating with such a wide range of people. The extensive possibilities for self-presentation are probably also attractive. It is also possible that some people are attracted by the *reduced* information available in this form of communication. Face-to-face communication is quite complex and some people find it daunting. Electronic communication can seem safer and more straightforward. Do not overdo it at the expense of other aspects of life.

Groups in the networked workplace

Even when the trends described above have gone to extremes, most workplaces contain a number of different social groups, both official and unofficial. This section will briefly describe the different kinds of group that exist and the functions they serve. We will suggest that these functions cannot yet be met by electronic communication alone.

Valid group functions

- To make decisions, or to accept decisions made elsewhere.
- To disseminate information.
- To validate individual's efforts. Group members should benefit from group appreciation of what they have accomplished.
- To provide constructive (not purely critical) feedback about individual accomplishments.
- To further a sense of mutual effort and team membership.
- To develop group standards, values and attitudes.
- To allow members to obtain moral support for their problems.

- To allow members to have normal social interactions with each other, discussing matters that have nothing to do with business.

Groups can be run 'too cold' in a manner which prevents all but the first two of these functions, although the remaining functions make the group more enjoyable and build a team which may work more effectively. We suggest that if these functions are not met by a team, then staff will tend to develop less formal groups to serve these functions, or if this is not possible then they will tend to feel isolated and to be less satisfied in their work.

The reason for this is that the two major causes of job satisfaction are feeling in control of one's own work and having the opportunity for normal social interactions (Neff, 1977). Somebody who literally works alone lacks the latter and, although technically in control of their own work, might not feel in control because their decisions are not socially-validated.

To an extent, these functions may be met by electronic groups, but it is probably difficult to deal with the more personal and emotive aspects of groups electronically, although this can be efficient for the exchange and dissemination of information. Formal and informal groups at work will tend to evolve to serve the functions listed above. In examining a workplace, it is important to look at the groups that actually exist, as well as those that exist officially.

Basic types of group at work

Teams

The workplace team can meet all the social and work needs of team members. As mentioned in Chapter 11, at the extreme this can be stressful for team members who may feel reluctant but obliged to socialise and under considerable pressure to get along with the team. In networked society, there can be ambiguity about team membership. Is the employee a member of the organisation's team of specialists on such-and-such a topic who are located all over the place but communicate regularly, or a worker in the local office? Both loyalties and management structures may be divided.

Committees and meetings

There are two opposing views of meetings. First, that they should be cold and businesslike, take as little time as possible and are primarily for making decisions. People's feelings should be dealt with elsewhere, if at all. Second, that meetings serve important social and emotional functions, should be warm and friendly, provide the opportunity for everyone to express themselves and are primarily for coming to terms with things. Decisions may be made elsewhere. There is a need for both sorts of function in organisations and if meetings are not run so that both functions are served – perhaps not always during the same meetings – then these functions will tend to occur elsewhere, perhaps informally. For example, if the only meetings are brief decision-making sessions where everyone stands up, then social and emotional functions may be met in the pub after work. On the other hand, if meetings never make decisions because so much time has been spent venting feelings, then decisions are liable to be made by individual managers without full consideration. Knowing whether your staff like or dislike something is not the same as analysing its costs and benefits.

Presentations

These are usually formal and concerned with the transmission of information. Any more emotive discussion will generally be relatively restrained and real feelings will be kept until later. It is therefore unusual for presentations to serve any functions but the dissemination of information. An exception is the motivational seminar, where a charismatic speaker aims to improve how the audience feels about themselves and their work. This may provide standards as to how the audience should feel and behave, but is likely to require additional group work to actually achieve beneficial changes in group activity. Formal and informal group discussions of the content of presentations can be more influential than the presentations themselves.

Co-workers

Despite the increase in working from home and 'on the move', most people still work at least some of the time in a place where there is a group of other people. This group may be a tightly-knit team (see Chapter 11), but it may also be simply a collection of people who work in the same place, perhaps even for different employers, as in a street market. Such groups may not be intended to be influential, but if day-to-day social relationships occur there, while formal management or team meetings occur only infrequently, then co-workers may exert great influence and informally work to goals that differ substantially from official organisational policies.

Informal social groupings

Staff can and do meet over lunch, smoking on the back door step and after work. The influence of these groups can be considerable, but many organisations neglect to consider this, other than vaguely referring to 'networking'. It can be during informal social groupings that essential information is exchanged, particularly information about the social structure of the organisation; in other words gossip. Goffman's (1968) concept of 'backstage' is also relevant. In informal groupings hierarchical distinctions may be relaxed and staff may be more willing to express feelings to each other. The role of alcohol as a social facilitator and disinhibitor is also important here. After a few drinks people can be more outspoken and less discrete, perhaps with the option of taking back their behaviour the next day; 'Sorry, I'd had too much to drink.' This sort of activity is probably essential to smooth and ease normal social relationships at work. Wise and progressive organisations ensure that there are regular opportunities for informal social groupings available to all staff, not just those who are willing and able to go to the pub after work (which may exclude people with families, women – if the pub is too traditional – and non-drinkers).

The need for socialising

It is no surprise to find us, as social psychologists, suggesting that socialising at work is not a waste of time. When more routine communications are remote and automated, then socialising may be even more important, as opportunities for these activities will diminish in the routine working day. You should appreciate the range of formal and informal groups that exist at work and realise that there are needs for social and emotional discussion that cannot be adequately satisfied by electronic communication, or very cold and formal group meetings.

Some people enjoy socialising in cyberspace, but we think that there are two major difficulties. First, the ability to manipulate the presentation of self in cyberspace makes interactions somewhat synthetic. Second, electronic interactions are highly impoverished compared to face-to-face or telephone communications. In cyberspace one can avoid getting any sense of the whole person at the other end of the communication. Not only may they have manipulated their self-presentation but you will only communicate about a limited range of topics – often only about some specific hobby or interest – and never see any of their incidental behaviour. Face-to-face interactions allow one to view leakage cues and to form opinions of others at a social distance, before committing to a further relationship. So far, such processes are difficult in cyberspace. Cyberspace may revolutionise our social lives and it may also develop richer ways of enabling interpersonal communication, but it is too early to tell.

Summary

To sum up, here are some key points about communication in networked society.

- The elite workers of the future are likely to be skilled users of cyberspace.
- More communication is automated and remote, but this does not facilitate the social and emotional aspects of communication.
- Most human activity in cyberspace is lurking.
- Most originated communications receive little or no reply.
- Group membership is always somewhat uncertain.
- Communication is usually asynchronous and threaded.
- Most communications in cyberspace are stored.
- Communication can be uninhibited and irresponsible compared to normal workplace communications.
- Electronic communications lack information relative to face-to-face ones and this can make effective interaction difficult.
- Face-to-face groups are still required, because they allow for more efficient discussion using the full range of verbal and non-verbal cues.
- Face-to-face groups also meet the social needs of staff that may not be readily met electronically.

Exercises

The content of discussion lists

If you can, connect to the internet and find a discussion list that interests you. Read over its archives. What proportion of messages are self-referential – about using the list, rather than having any content? What proportion of messages show too much emotionality? What proportion show too little? Is there real multi-way discussion on the list, or do people simply post messages that are rarely followed-up?

Chat

If you can, connect to the internet and find a chat room that interests you. Try and strike up a conversation and see how you get on.
What conversational ploys worked? Were you able to get beyond
banalities? Did you feel that you were 'really talking' to other people?

Recommended reading

Brotherton, C. (1999), *Social Psychology and Management*, Milton Keynes:
    Open University Press.
Castells, M. (1996–1998) *The Information Age: Economy, Society and Culture*,
    vols. 1–3, Oxford: Blackwell.
Preece, J., Rogers, Y., Sharp, H., Benyon, D., Holland, S. and Carey, T.
    (1994) *Human–Computer Interaction*, Harlow: Addison-Wesley.
Suler, J. (1999) *The Psychology of Cyberspace*, Department of Psychology,
    Rider University. http://www.rider.edu/users/suler/psycyber/psycyber.html

13 Summing up

By now you should realise that group communication is both the most natural and most complex of human activities. People are social beings and are influenced by group processes far more than some care to admit. We have seen that it can be helpful to be more observant and aware of these processes in the workplace, to be more reflective about how you present yourself at work, and how others present themselves, and to understand how to converse appropriately with other people. It may also be helpful to appreciate the extent to which your identity is shaped by and shapes the groups that you work in. It is important to appreciate the power of individual and group narratives to form a world-view that will have major effects on the nature of your work.

Effective groups at work tend to have appropriate world-views that are functional, reasonable and capable of change – that is, evidence-based. This flexibility is particularly important as the rate of change in society speeds up. It is also important that new groups can be formed quickly and work together effectively. For this, it is vital that the emotional and social needs of a group are considered as well as their rational workplace functions. Among these needs are that everybody can be heard. It is also important to understand how group pressures can affect individual behaviour and particularly to accept that this applies to everybody, including yourself and the present authors.

Groups are the main venue for decision-making and negotiation at work, but group processes and dynamics can hinder effective work, or lead to poor, even disastrous, outcomes. Groups at work can function well socially, even too well, and hence come to a shared, but dysfunctional, irrational or rigid view of the world that causes problems. Again, it is easy to accept this for others, but it applies to everyone. Teams in the workplace can be regarded as ideal, well-functioning groups with clearly defined roles. Although there are some disadvantages to team working, there are also important benefits and it is particularly helpful to realise that different characters and working styles can benefit a workplace. A highly conformist group, where all members are very similar, is unlikely to be effective or adaptable. Adaptability will continue to be a key organisational skill as network society continues to develop. The role of computer-mediated communications will continue to expand and it will be interesting to see how this influences group communication and styles of working.

Organisations that continue to ignore group processes in the workplace, or simply muddle along with whatever practices have evolved naturally, risk losing competitive advantage.

Notes

3 Non-verbal channels of communication

1 However, in face-preserving situations if asked the transmitter may continue to deny any problem. Instead, the receiver is expected to produce the face-preserving solution.

6 The social construction of identity

1 Received English is an ideal rather than something that people actually speak – it uses standard English grammar and what sounds like neutral pronunciation; BBC English was something like this before dialect speakers were welcomed as presenters.

2 This may sound critical of families. It is not, for what else can they do? Taking drastic measures, such as terminating relationships with the drinker, can make some people sober up, but it makes things even worse for other drinkers and gives them even more freedom to drink. How bad do things have to get before drastic measures are called for? There are no simple answers; many families put up with much more from their members than they would ever have expected to.

7 The formation of groups

1 For example, the managing director of a company might believe that he makes all the decisions, while his staff are actually operating the company as part of a network without his full awareness.

2 We are not suggesting that this is a good hiring practice. It probably is not (Byrne, 1990).

3 There may also be other reasons for such behaviour, including that their feelings are not being acknowledged (see Chapter 3) and that they are serving unconscious group needs (see earlier in this chapter).

4 We accept that many religions provide rules whose alleged origin is God. Nonetheless fallible people interpret these rules, so our point applies to them also. Indeed if the divine word seems stupid or inappropriate, surely it has been misunderstood?

8 Social influence in groups

1 Gossip also serves to provide normal social interactions at work, and to consolidate group norms.

11 Teams and roles

1 Corporate mission statements are often indistinctive and general. For example most British universities have mission statements that include the words 'education', 'research' and either 'quality' or 'excellence'.

12 Group communications in networked society

1 A good starting place for some of the web's stranger sites is the Center for the Easily Amused (http//www.cea.com), one of whose designers apparently just turned 18 during 1999.

References

Adams, S. (1997) *The Dilbert Principle*, London: Boxtree.

Adler, R.B and Towne, N. (1993) *Looking Out / Looking In*, seventh edition, Fort Worth: Harcourt Brace Jovanovich.

Asch, S.E. (1955) Opinions and social pressure. *Scientific American*, 193, 31–55.

Asch, S.E. (1956) Studies of independence and conformity: A minority of one against a unanimous majority. *Psychological Monographs*, 70 (9) entire issue 416.

Bandura, A (1977) *Social Learning Theory*, Englewood Cliffs, NJ: Prentice-Hall.

Belbin, R.M. (1981) *Management Teams – Why They Succeed or Fail*, Oxford: Heinemann.

Berne, E. (1964) *Games People Play: The Psychology of Human Relationships*, London: Penguin.

Bion, W.R. (1961) *Experiences in Groups and Other Papers*, London: Tavistock.

Birdwhistell, R. (1970) *Kinesis and Context*, Philadelphia: University of Pennsylvania Press.

Brotherton, C. (1999) *Social Psychology and Management*, Milton Keynes: Open University Press.

Brown, R. (1996) *Group Processes: Dynamics Within and Between Groups*, Oxford: Blackwell.

Buchanan, A. (1996) *Cycles of Child Maltreatment: Facts, Fallacies and Interventions*, Chichester: Wiley.

Byrne, K. (1990) *Hiring: Strategies For Success*, Brighton: Victoria, Wright-books.

Castells, M. (1998) *The Information Age: Economy, Society and Culture*, volumes 1–3, Oxford: Blackwell.

Costa, P.T. Jr and McCrae, R.R. (1992) '"Set like plaster?" Evidence for the stability of adult personality', in T. Heatherton and J. Weinberger (eds) *Can Personality Change?*, Washington, DC: American Psychological Association.

Dillon, J. (1997) 'Questioning', in O. Hargie (ed.) *The Handbook of Communication Skills*, second edition, London: Routledge.

Dimbleby, R. and Burton, G. (1992) *More Than Words. An Introduction to Communication*, second edition, London: Routledge.

Dion, K.K., Berscheid, E. and Walster, E. (1972) What is beautiful is good. *Journal of Personality and Social Psychology*, 24, 285–90.

Dryden, W. (1996) *Inquiries in Rational Emotive Behaviour Therapy*, London: Sage.

Ellis, R. and McClintock, A. (1991) *If You Take My Meaning: Theory into Practice in Human Communication*, London: Edward Arnold.

English, S. and Yazdani, M. (1999) Computer-supported cooperative learning in a virtual university. *Journal of Computer Assisted Learning*, 15, 2–13.

Forgas, J. P. (1985) *Interpersonal Behaviour; The Psychology of Social Interaction*, Sydney: Pergamon Press.

Forgas, J.P., O'Connor, K. and Morris, S. (1983) Smile and punishment: The effects of facial expression on responsibility attribution by groups and individuals. *Personality and Social Psychology Bulletin*, 9, 587–96.

Foulkes, S.H. (1964) *Therapeutic Group Analysis*, New York: International Universities Press.

Fraser, C., Gouge, C. and Billig, M. (1971) Risky shifts, cautious shifts, and group polarization. *European Journal of Social Psychology*, 1, 7–30.

Freud, S. (1921) 'Group psychology and the analysis of the ego', in S. Freud (1985) *Civilisation, Society and Religion*, volume 12, Pelican Freud Library, Harmondsworth: Penguin.

Garfinkel, H. (1967) *Studies in Ethnomethodology*, Englewood Cliffs, NJ: Prentice-Hall.

Goffman, E. (1959) *The Presentation of Self in Everyday Life*, Harmondsworth: Pelican.

Goffman, E. (1963) *Stigma*, Englewood Cliffs, NJ: Prentice-Hall.

Goffman, E. (1968) *Asylums: Essays on the Social Situation of Mental Patients and Other Inmates*, Harmondsworth: Penguin. (First published 1961.)

Griffiths, M. (1999) Internet addiction: Fact or fiction? *The Psychologist*, 12, 5, 246–50.

Handy, C.B. (1985) *Understanding Organizations*, New York: Facts on File.

Hargie, O.D.W. (1997) *The Handbook of Communication Skills*, second edition, London: Routledge.

Harré, R. and Lamb, R. (eds) (1986) *The Dictionary of Personality and Social Psychology*, Oxford: Blackwell.

Hartley, P. (1997) *Group Communication*, London: Routledge.

Hirokawa, R. (1988) 'Group communication research: Considerations for the use of interaction analysis', in C. H. Tardy (ed.) *A Handbook for the Study of Human Communication: Methods and Instruments for Observing, Measuring and Assessing Communication Process*, Norwood NG: Ablex.

Holdaway, S. (1997) Creating and sustaining race within the police workforce. *British Journal of Sociology*, 48, 19–34.

Horton, M. (1999) 'Working with groups', in D. Messer and F. Jones (eds) *Psychology and Social Care*, London: Jessica Kingsley.

Horwitz, M. and Rabbie, J.M. (1982) 'Individuality and membership in the intergroup system', in H. Tajfel (ed.) *Social Identity and Intergroup Relations*, Cambridge: Cambridge University Press.

Ivey, A. and Authier, J. (1978) *Micro-counselling: Innovations in interviewing, counselling, psychotherapy and psychoeducation*, Springfield, IL: C.C. Thomas.

Janis, I. (1982) *Victims of Groupthink: A Psychological Study of Foreign Policy Decisions and Fiascos*, second edition, Boston, MA: Houghton Mifflin.

Janis, I.L. and Mann, L. (1977) *Decision Making*, New York: Free Press.

Jenkins, R. (1996) *Social Identity*, London: Routledge.

Jourard, S.M. (1971) *Self-disclosure: An Experimental Analysis of the Transparent Self*, New York: Wiley-Interscience.

Kahn, R.L. and Cannell, C.F. (1957) *The Dynamics of Interviewing*, New York: Wiley.

Katzenbach, J.R. and Smith, D.K. (1993) *The Wisdom of Teams*, Cambridge, MA: Harvard Business School.

Kogan, N. and Wallach, M.A. (1964) *Risk Taking: A Study in Cognition and Personality*, New York: Holt, Rinehart and Winston.

Lacan, J. (1979) The Four Fundamental Concepts of Psychoanalysis, Harmondsworth: Penguin.

Lewin, K. (1948) *Resolving Social Conflicts*, New York: Harper and Row.

Luft, J. and Ingham, H. (1955) *The Johari Window: A Graphic Model for Interpersonal Relationships*, Berkeley: University of California, Western Training Laboratory in Group Development.

McAdams, D.P. (1993) *Stories We Live By. Personal Myths and the Making of the Self*, New York: Morrow.

McCrae, R.R. (ed.) (1992) The five-factor model: Issues and applications (Special Issue). *Journal of Personality*, 60, (2), entire issue.

McKenna, E. (1998) *Business Psychology and Organisational Behaviour*, Hove, UK: Psychology Press.

Merleau-Ponty, M. (1962) *Phenomenology of Perception*, London, Routledge and Kegan Paul.

Milgram, S. (1974) *Obedience and Authority: An Experimental View*, London: Tavistock.

Moreland, R.L. and Levine, J.M. (1994) *Understanding Small Groups*, Boston, MA: Allyn and Bacon.

Moscovici, S. and Zavalloni, M. (1969) The group as a polarizer of attitudes. *Journal of Personality and Social Psychology*, 12, 125–35.

Neff, W.S. (1977) *Work and Human Behavior*, Chicago: Aldine.

Nelson-Jones, R. (1983) *Practical Counselling Skills*, Eastbourne: Holt Rinehart Winston.

Niven, N. (1994) *Health Psychology*, second edition, Edinburgh: Churchill Livingstone.

Orne, M.T. (1962) On the social psychology of the psychological experiment: with particular reference to demand characteristics and their implications. *American Psychologist*, 17, 776–83.

Preece, J., Rogers, Y., Sharp, H., Benyon, D., Holland, S. and Carey, T. (1994) *Human-Computer Interaction*, Harlow: Addison-Wesley.

Rabbie, J.M. and Horwitz, M. (1969) Arousal of ingroup–outgroup bias by a chance win or loss. *Journal of Personality and Social Psychology*, 13, 269–77.

Roethlisberger, F. and Dickson, W. (1939) *Management and the Worker*, Cambridge, MA: Harvard University Press.

Rungapadiachy, D.M. (1999) *Interpersonal Communication and Psychology for Health Care Professionals*, Oxford: Butterworth Heinemann.

Robins, L.N. and Rutter, M. (eds) (1990) *Straight and Devious Pathways from Childhood to Adulthood*, Cambridge: Cambridge University Press.

Sapsford, R., Still, A., Wetherell, M., Miell, D. and Stevens, R. (eds) (1998) *Theory and Social Psychology*, London: Sage.

Sherif, M. (1935) A study of some social factors in perception. *Archives of Psychology*, 187.

Sherif, M. and Sherif, C.W. (1969) *Social Psychology*, New York: Harper and Row.

Sobel, D. (1996) *Longitude*, London: Fourth Estate.

Steiner, I.D. (1972) *Group Processes and Productivity*, New York: Academic Press.

Stevenage, S.A. and McKay, Y. (1999) Model applicants: The effect of facial appearance on recruitment decisions. *British Journal of Psychology*, 90, 221–34.

Stoner, J.A.F. (1961) 'A comparison of individuals and group decisions involving risk', in D. C. Pennington (ed.) (1986) *Essential Social Psychology*, London: Edward Arnold.

Suler, J. (1999) *The Psychology of Cyberspace*, Department of Psychology, Rider University. http://www.rider.edu/users/suler/psycyber/psycyber.html

Susman, E.B. (1998) Cooperative learning: A review of factors that increase the effectiveness of cooperative computer-based instruction. *Journal of Educational Computing Research*, 18, 303–22.

Sutherland, S. (1992) *Irrationality*, London: Penguin.

Tajfel, H. (1981) *Human Groups and Social Categories*, Cambridge: Cambridge University Press.

Tolman, C.W. (1994) *Psychology, Society and Subjectivity. An Introduction to German Critical Psychology*, London: Routledge.

Tuckman, B. (1965) Developmental sequence in small groups. *Psychological Bulletin*, 63, 384–99.

Tuckman, B.W. and Jensen, M.A. (1977) Stages in small group development revisited. *Group and Organisational Studies*, 2, 419–27.

Turner, J. (1987) *Rediscovering the Social Group*, Oxford: Blackwell.

Vonk, R. (1999) Differential evaluations of likeable and dislikeable behaviours enacted towards superiors and subordinates. *European Journal of Social Psychology*, 29, 139–46.

Wech, B.A., Mossholder, K.W., Steel, R.P. and Bennett, N. (1998) Does work group cohesiveness affect individuals' performance and organizational commitment? A cross-level examination. *Small Group Research*, 29, 472–94.

Wellings, R.S. (1994) 'Building a self-directed work team', in C. Mabey and P. Iles (eds) *Managing Learning*, London: Routledge.

Wicker, A.W. (1984) *An Introduction to Ecological Psychology*, Cambridge: Cambridge University Press.

Wit, A.P. and Wilke, H.A.M. (1997) 'Interacting in task groups', in O. Hargie (ed.) *The Handbook of Communication Skills*, second edition, London: Routledge.

Woodcock, M. (1979) *Team Development Manual*, London: Gower.

Yalom, I.D. (1985) *The Theory and Practice of Group Psychotherapy*, New York: Basic Books.

Zimbardo, P. (1969) 'The human choice: individuation, reason and order versus deindividuation, impulse and chaos', in W.J. Arnold and D. Levine (eds) *Nebraska Symposium on Motivation*, volume 17. Lincoln: University of Nebraska Press, pp. 237–307.

Zimbardo, P.G., Haney, C., Banks, W. and Jaffe, D. (1973) A Pirandellian prison: The mind is a formidable jailer. *New York Times Magazine* 8 April, 38–60.

Zimbardo, P., McDermott, M., Jansz, J. and Metaal, N. (1995) *Psychology. A European Text*, London: HarperCollins.

Index